£2 22

Soft Lad

Soft Lad

A collection of stories (about me)

Nick Grimshaw

HODDER

First published in Great Britain in 2022 by Hodder & Stoughton
An Hachette UK company

1

Copyright © Nick Grimshaw 2022

The right of Nick Grimshaw to be identified as the Author of the
Work has been asserted by him in accordance with the Copyright, Designs
and Patents Act 1988.

Edited by Laura Weir

A CIP catalogue record for this title is available from the British Library

Hardback ISBN 978 1 399 70330 7
eBook ISBN 978 1 399 70331 4

Typeset in Electra by Hewer Text UK Ltd

Printed and bound in Great Britain by Clays Ltd, Elcograf S.p.A.

Hodder & Stoughton policy is to use papers that are natural, renewable
and recyclable products and made from wood grown in sustainable forests.
The logging and manufacturing processes are expected to conform to the
environmental regulations of the country of origin.

Hodder & Stoughton Ltd
Carmelite House
50 Victoria Embankment
London EC4Y 0DZ

www.hodder.co.uk

I'd like to dedicate this book to the ever funny, ever brilliant and ever supportive Eileen & Pete, my loving parents who made this soft lad who he is today

Contents

Introduction

I really thought I wanted to write a book. But thinking and doing are two very different things. I honestly believed I'd be able to knock it out in a week or so, cross-legged on the couch with a fag à la Carrie Bradshaw. But it was actually far more annoying, incredibly even more annoying than Carrie Bradshaw herself. Like Carrie, it was hard work and overly emotional. I'd have days reverting to stroppy teenage me, throwing myself on the couch in a tantrum, screaming into the sofa to muffle my maddening rage from the neighbours. 'FUCK THIS FUCKING BOOK,' I'd say to myself as I stomped downstairs to the makeshift office I'd made at the dining table.

The intention was there, the hope of becoming an author was there, everything was there apart from the main element of a book: words. Most of the writing processes in my brain from myself to myself went like this:

I'm more of a night owl, I'll do it tonight. I should get some sleep, I'll be better first thing. Do you think I can get out of this? How, seriously, could I get out of this? It's not me, it's the book. Maybe I'll start a different book now?

I'd start writing other things and bits that were nothing to do with me or what I'd intended to write about in *Soft Lad*. The questions got more abstract:

What even *is* a book? Do people even read books? WOW A BOOK IS A WEIRD THING – JUST SOME THINGS WRITTEN DOWN BY SOMEONE. MAD!

There was so much noise going in my brain about NOT doing it that I was exhausted by 10 a.m. And that's even before I got to doing any actual writing. I started making notes with my laptop and soon found I liked the old-fashioned pen and paper, opting for a professional Stella Artois pen as my quill.

I'd sit and think about people reading this book and it turned my stomach. Ughhhh, everyone is going to hate this and people will be so annoyed they bothered to buy it, it will all be my fault then I'll have to pay the publisher loads of money back cos everyone will have taken it back demanding a refund cos it's so crap and now they and probably Waterstones will be bankrupt and it will be this crummy book's fault.

It loomed over me like an STI test result. The result will be bad. Terminal. It will come out and people will protest, their hate for my book going into overdrive, them seeing red, starting to hate books as a concept and committing book mass murders by torching their local libraries.

Or maybe no one will notice. That would be nice. It will come out. My mum will like it and then no one will ever mention it again to me.

In writing this, I ascended to a new level of procrastination. I reached out to old friends, asked if neighbours needed help with anything, organised the spare room. Oh, maybe I should make a smoothie! I signed up for a bootcamp thinking the exercise would help my brain. I embarked on a new 12-step skincare routine, layering up all the products with a five-minute break in between each, nicely wasting a good forty-five minutes a day. I started walking the dogs so often that they're now the dog equivalents of Gladiators – all muscly and ripped from an overactive workout schedule.

I'd sit and argue with myself about the content: 'Am I talking about myself too much?' before realising, 'it's your fucking book, dickhead, who the fuck else are you going to talk about?'

My due date was February 2022, which sounded so futuristic when it was given to me in 2021 that it was like something in a sci-fi film. 2022! That's ages away! I might be dead by then! I'll do a little every day and then it will be done WELL before then! That did not happen.

I was putting it off but I didn't quite know why. Every other job in my life I can get on with, but this self-governed pressure I hated. My hate for it seeped out into my daily life and made everything seem overwhelmingly annoying: ughhhh I have to stop for lunch, uuughhh I have to have a Zoom, uuuuughhh I need to send an email but I'm writing Goddd, uughhh – it put me in a shitty mood.

But why? It was not my first day of work, so I struggled to figure out what was doing my head in so much about it.

It wasn't the concept of work that was the problem; I love nothing more than my agent cracking the whip so that I work all the hours God sends, I'm used to late nights, early starts and being so busy that I forget to eat lunch and feel all businessy like Lord Sugar. In the past I'd never been afraid of hard work – quite the opposite; my vision of what I wanted my job to be was totally clear and it was a long and hard path to get there. The problem wasn't the hard work. The problem was bigger than the work. It was me. I didn't want to invest in myself, I didn't want to think about myself, I didn't want to remember the old me or think about the new me or figure out who the hell 'me' even was. I didn't want to face myself. It felt too big, too real and too weird. It all felt a bit ME ME ME LISTEN TO ME! Maybe I'm shy, I thought. (He says, writing 70,000 words about himself.)

As loud as I am, I'm a realist when it comes to myself. I'm annoying, I know. Every time someone said, 'Yer shit on the radio,' I'd be like, well fair's fair. It felt like too much emotional hard work. Not the writing, not the research but the reflection. Did I really want to sit and think about my standing in the world, how I feel, how I felt, what I've done with my life? No, I didn't. I wanted to order e-cigs and Lotus biscuits and talk about something more important, like Megan Thee Stallion.

In my pit of procrastination, I realised I have this chip in my brain, and one on my shoulder, about success. And how I think I don't deserve it. I'm really good at attempting to fuck it all up. The inability to say no to a night out, the one more drink, the horrendous timekeeping so I'm in a perennial late mess state, one quick doughnut before bed even though I've been working out all day, leaving a suit at the dry-cleaners that I need that evening til 5.59 p.m. Why do I do this to myself? Like girl, give yourself a chance!

I knoooowwwww it would be easier and better to do it beforehand. So why leave it? A safety net I set up. So if anything is a failure, I have caused that failure myself. I can own my own failure. 'Like, well yeh it was shit because I didn't do anything, BUT if I did, it would be great.' Quite a shit mantra. JUST MAKE IT GREAT THEN YOU DUMB-DUMB.

While this was raging on in my head I'd take my fifth break of the day and watch *The Kardashians*. Let's see what salads they're eating in their museum-sized kitchens today. Usually their boring kitchens and boring salads weirdly motivate me as I thank Jesus that I don't live in Calabasas, and revel in the go-go-go-ness of London life. But even these fuckers are up in the gym at 5 a.m. with Kris taking business calls and going on til midnight. Right! Kris wouldn't stand for this shit . . . get the fucking thing wrote.

I had to sort it out. I had a plan, I'd write every day, nine to five, then treat myself to a nice tea each night. I set an alarm for six thirty every morning and titled it something so cringe I can't believe I'm saying it – get your sickbags ready – 'DO IT FOR YOU'. My very own motivational mantra that I'd see first thing, as soon as I open my eyes, to make me jump out of the bed with a self-worthy spring in my step.

It didn't work once. Not one single time. I'd snooze and snooze with 'DOOO ITTT FOORRR YOUUU' flashing up as I whispered 'fuck off' and shook my dozy head back to sleep.

That was of course unless I had to be up for someone else. A TV show commitment, a meeting, filming, anything else I'd be right up, out of bed, downstairs like Mary Poppins, ready for the day ahead.

Now that I had something to do for me, I'd be sat at the dining table doing some life admin, check in on everyone I know. I wasted time by calling my friend Aimee and whinging, saying I wish I'd done something with my life. She'd remind me I did, I famously accomplished my childhood dream, found love and was now getting married and I'm meant to be writing a book about it. She didn't understand. 'What do you want then? What's the solution here?' she asked. I didn't know what I wanted. All I knew was that I didn't want to write this crummy book: enjoying it so far, guys?

I saw this time at home 'writing' as a time to be Mother Teresa, fixing everyone else's problems. I spend a lot of time trying to make other people feel OK. Making sure all Uber drivers get five stars even if their farts made me gag and they inexplicably dropped me ten doors away from my house. My time as a soft lad out in these streets equipped me with a superhero level of compassion and I'm racked with guilt on the way back from the shops at the thought of accidently not smiling back at a smiling old lady who now might now be sad that a man didn't smile back at her. I worry the dogs are depressed, when really they're just sleeping. I worry I should have given the homeless man money rather than a sandwich. But I'm just an arsehole to myself. My internal monologue is Maleficent.

One day I decided it had to stop. I had to write this book. Not for me, not for you, but for my publisher – she's pregnant you see and if I don't send stuff she will be stressed and then the baby will be stressed and grow up stressed and IT WILL ALL BE MY FAULT. The unborn baby of a lady I email does not need my shit. Right, get on with it, I thought!

First, I should meditate. Get me grounded. Get the baby this lady I've met three times is having far away from the stress. I've always had an attention issue and an anxiety issue so in lockdown I was told to meditate. I learnt over Zoom with ponytailed DJ and festival nomad Rob Da Bank. And occasionally when anxiety was sky-high or when I needed to procrastinate or when I should be writing a book, I'd participate.

This was the first perfect distraction of the day. I sat in the lounge in silence. I'd light and waft around some palo santo, unclear what it does but I'd seen it on Instagram so it seemed legit. I'd close my eyes, relax my shoulders and attempt to just 'be'. I could maybe make it to around one whole minute before I'd get interrupted. Not by my partner Mesh or the dogs or a noisy neighbour, but – you guessed it – by my own disruptive brain. Even as I'm doing the one thing proven over millennia to help people be grounded and more centred in themselves, I'd find myself distracted. I was no longer thinking of my soul, or my third eye, or just being. I was, every time, distracted thinking about pop princess Dua Lipa. I'd sit there cross-legged, and sing to the tune of her mega-hit 'Levitating':

'I'M MEDITATING!'

Meditation over. Fucking Dua fucking Lipa and her incredible pop work! Ruining this book! Ruining my life! My zenness! And stressing out that poor woman at the publishing company! And her poor baby! Nice one Dua Lipa!

Weeks passed and I lied to myself about how good my book was coming on. I thought after I left Radio 1 I'd have more time and space for reflection. Space for a deep dive, a breather on daily life and be able to sit and think about what I want to say to the world. It was crickets. I needed a break. A creative reset, time to let my brain recalibrate after the realisation that my full life's focus until that point, my childhood dream of radio, was over. So I decided a month in LA would be what was needed. It's far away, it's sunny, it's a city, we can do things in the evenings and I can write all day . . .

I didn't write all day. I didn't write at all.

I got back to London and saw my friend Drew, who was in town from New York. Drew is like a very cute rescue dog, in that I can't wait to see him and he's adorably cute but at any moment SNAP he could bite your hand off. He's a textbook New Yorker, plays hard but works even harder, sassed up to the max with a sharp tongue to match his even sharper outfits.

The evening started delightfully with dinner and Drew laughed along but as we headed to his hotel room, he cut to the chase. He asked me what I was up to, and I was scared to mention the book. He's a doer and I tend to think I'm not a doer. Even though I have . . . done. Drew has an intensity that only New Yorkers seem to have. A self-awareness or is it a super-professionalism? I don't know but we don't have it drilled into us as Brits. When I told the rest of my friends in England about this book they'd go, 'lol, you, write a book?' or, 'Are ya havin' a party for it then? Can I come?' Whereas Drew wanted to dive deep.

'Well . . .' I say.

'An autobiography?' he asks.

'No, no, it's not an autobiography.'

'Right, so what is it?' The New York abruptness that I love really starting to come to the boil now.

'Well, it's a collection of stories . . . about me,' I say.

Drew sips on his vape, sunglasses firmly on indoors. '. . . Riiiiiiight?' he says.

He's giving *The Devil Wears Prada* levels of friendliness.

'So *why* are you writing it?' he says.

I can feel myself starting to panic. I make a joke with our dinner pal Aimee about it being for the cash.

He doesn't like it. Drew likes to prefix the big questions by announcing he has a question and I dread it with all my heart. He goes, 'Here's a question . . .'

Here we go, I think. The question is bubbling up inside of me before I've even heard it, it's going to be a juicy one, I just know it.

'Why is it important?' he asks and stares deep into me, exhaling a puff of vape. He knows it's a good question.

Ah shit. I don't know.

'I dunno, because it's lol?' I say. Aimee and I chuckle before we are interrupted —

'NO! No, no. WHY is it important?' he asks, this time somehow even more sternly.

I say, 'Eerrrrmmmmmmmmmmmmmmm' for roughly forty-five seconds.

Truth is, I didn't know why it was important. Mainly because I didn't think it *was* important. And maybe because I don't think of myself being important? Fucking hell, Drew, what a question!

I know some people are scared of Drew. He can be abrupt, hard, brutally honest. So when he washed up on UK soil to see us I wasn't mentally ready for this Emily Maitlis-level grilling. We don't talk like that here. I've had friends say to Drew, 'I don't like my job.'

Drew would drop an emotionless 'Why?'

'I don't like my department.'

'Change then,' he'd say.

'It's not that easy.'

'Why?' he'd say.

'Because of my boss.'

'Become the boss,' he'd say.

Whereas in the UK we'd just go, 'Yer boss is a bitch, fuck it, let's get pissed!'

But when I was trapped in his hotel room with that big fucking question looming over me, I didn't exactly enjoy the experience.

'I'll tell you why it's important,' he said.

'It is important because you, as a queer, weird kid in the suburbs who was hanging around with your elderly neighbours, being obsessed with making a racket and playing music as loud as it would go, had laser-sharp vision of what you wanted to do with your life.

'And then . . . you actually did it. You made it happen.

'And THAT IS why it's important. You had a dream, you had the vision and you stuck to your guns and YOU made it come true. So let the children know. For all the little queer kids feeling left out in suburbia, feeling not at the centre of the party, they can make their own party. They need to know that life is what you make it and you made it what you wanted.'

I'm left, for once, speechless. I sit there in awe at this slice of 1 a.m. real talk. Hey! That did happen! I think. I'll go home and write now! Or maybe just get Drew to do it?

The next morning I thought of little me, the little kid who shuddered at the thought of being called a soft lad, and I wondered how he'd feel about SOFT LAD being emblazoned across a book that the future him had written. I wrote and wrote for hours to help the publisher's unborn baby be born stress-free and so Drew wouldn't shout at me or ask me any more real life questions. But mainly for all the soft lads out there. I always thought I hated being called a 'soft lad'. I saw it as a diss, something to be ashamed of. But, try as I might, I am a soft lad. It's who I am. Here's how the softness shaped me.

1

Dying for Attention

Growing up there were a few nights of TV that really got me going: *The Brits*, *The Royal Variety Performance*, *Children In Need* – but Comic Relief night was where my televisual event-watching hit its peak. It felt MONUMENTAL and anyone who was anyone was talking about it – Mrs Bebb at school, Anthea Turner on *Blue Peter*, Auntie Carmel . . . I mean, for six-year-old me it was everything, the event of the year, my very own Met Gala. I'd talk about it for weeks on end, begging to be taken to WHSmith in the Manchester Arndale for a red nose, where I could drop my quid into the box and save the world. I'd wear it from the minute I woke up, stomping down all proud and charitable in my PJs, before attempting to delicately chow down some Cinnamon Grahams without knocking it off into my milky bowl below. My human nose would never really manage to hold on to the red nose and I'd endure the walk to school with my head angled upwards towards the sky, half from a sense of pride in my charitable display and half in a battle against gravity. My nose was pinched so tightly I talked like I had a heavy cold, all in a bid to be part of this magical night of wonder. The impending sense of occasion ran through me like electricity, it was all I could talk and think about and I'd rally round the family, excitedly telling them, 'It's Comic Relief three weeks on Friday!! OMMGGGGGGGGSOOOOOEXCITEDDDDDAREYOU? AREYOU??'

They weren't but I never wanted to watch it alone. I had to make it into an evening spectacular, and saw that my part of the Comic Relief mission was to recruit the entire family to the cause. Mum and Dad were easily on board – 'All right, all right we know' when I'd excitedly count down the days to them each morning as if it was actual Christmas.

Our Andrew and Our Jane were less up for it. They were both teenagers and rightly mortified at staying in on a Friday night with their parents and baby brother watching someone like Richard Madeley get gunged. They allegedly had better things to do. And I was furious about it. I was totally obsessed with them so I hated them going out on Friday nights and leaving me home alone with boring Eileen and Pete – aka Mum and Dad – but especially on Comic Relief night!

I'd beg them to stay and watch, physically dragging them to the TV by their sleeves with all my body weight pulled against them. Shoving them into chairs, I'd sit on the paisley-print carpeted floor cross-legged with the volume on 100. It would be the one night where I'd have charge of the remote and deliver SSSSSHHHH's to anyone daring to pass anything other than a positive comment on the show. Around me I'd have two bowls of crisps and a side plate with six carefully placed Viscount biscuits, their green metal foil covers glistening, adding a touch of glam to the evening's events.

'LOOK LOOK LOOK, your money can help change the lives of others,' I'd say, reading from the screen. I could sense the room wasn't as up for it as I was . . .

Our Jane would half-arsedly watch with me for a bit. I'd know she wasn't staying as I could smell she had perfume on, she'd be there in her dungarees and Palladium trainers, long hair hanging over her face to her waist, before saying, 'I'm going to my mate's, you watch with Mum.'

'You're gonna miss the best bit! The newsreaders are about to put 'Lady Marmalade' sexy clothes on and do karaoke!!' I'd scream out into the hall from the lounge.

Her loss, I'd think with a tut as I turned back to the screen, my audience rapidly declining.

My trickiest customer in my great bid to watch though was Our Andrew. He liked rap, terrifying electronic music and telling me to fuck off a lot. He didn't conform to society, he didn't care for primetime TV nor did he think Dawn French was funny – in fact he thought she was 'shit'.

Now this exclamation shocked me to my core. One step too far, I thought, Dawn French NOT funny? He's got her confused or missed the joke, I thought. I was appalled at his lack of excitement for a charitable comedy gala! 'Do you not care about helping others?' I'd ask.

At six foot three he was a giant to me and his words took on an almighty power to my juvenile bowl-haired self. 'You wanna be more worried about the power of capitalism and this government trying to water down youth culture and brainwash you lot to enjoy this dirge on the TV . . .'.

'But it's so funny, Lenny Henry is KILLING it out there!' I'd argue back.

'Your problem is that you're a marketeer's dream,' he'd say.

'Ah thanks!' I'd say, not fully understanding him but knowing 'dream' sounded quite nice.

My six-year-old self was totally dumbstruck and slightly saddened for him that he DIDN'T want to take part in THE BIGGEST NIGHT ON TV. 'But they're doing an *Ab Fab* special!' I said as he slammed the door in my face singing 'Fight the Power' and making DJ scratching noises with his mouth.

Comic Relief fell on a Friday and Fridays meant Gran Beattie would come over for tea, Dad would go to the chippy and I'd beg to eat it in the lounge on special occasions like tonight. I'd love it when Gran Beattie watched TV with me as she was less likely to be popping her leather jacket on and running off to a rave like my siblings, so she was more easily manipulated by little me. I'd keep one eye on the screen and one on Beattie, making sure she was watching. Occasionally she'd turn her head to glance down at the paper or look out the window and I'd forcibly turn her ancient head with both hands and say, 'GRAN! AREYAWATCINNNN?! WATCH ALI G!' She was born in 1912, the nuances of a rap parody were lost on her.

I'd settle for watching with the olds and I'd make it to a KER-RAZY 10.30 p.m. before passing out on the sofa and then waking up the next day in bed. 'How much did we raise??' as soon as my eyes opened, feeling a sense of pride, thinking I'd saved the world by watching telly.

I'd float around the next day like you do after a wedding, still high on the excitement of the night before. It felt like the world had been watching, that I was part of something, something really exciting. The anything-could-happen energy wound me up something rotten and the live-and-looseness of it all compared to our usual telly viewings of *Corrie* and *The Krypton Factor* felt wildly rebellious. The funny bits made me piss my pants laughing, with the sad sights of extreme poverty making me choke up, confused as to why all these plastic red nose purchases hadn't stopped world hunger already. It wasn't just the lols I loved; the show was important to me. It showed me the live, rough-and-ready school of presenting, it introduced me to the shared experience of telly and it's where I first experienced human compassion. It mattered to me, it opened my eyes to others, and seeing how others lived fascinated me. I felt we all had to do what we could to help. So years later when I was asked to trek 100 miles across Outer Mongolia to raise money for Comic Relief I just couldn't say no.

Apart from I did.

See, the challenge was for Sport Relief not Comic Relief and, if I'm honest, sport just isn't for me. Just saying the word makes me retch. Ew! It's so macho, competitive and skilled. All the things I am not. I've managed to swerve away from sport with such dexterity that ironically, I could be awarded some sort of sporting medal for doing so. It's a word drenched in dread for me, it's something I don't partake in privately, nor is it something I'd be eager to do on the television.

My relationship with sport couldn't be more fair-weather – I like Héctor Bellerín's haircuts and I'll dabble when it's the Euros and we can all go to the pub at 2 p.m. on a Tuesday and sing in the street but apart from that it's a no from me. I did spend a lot of time on the tennis court at school. Not with a ball and racket but with a ten-pack of Sovereigns, which retailed at £1.45 back in the heady 90s. In my teenage bid to embody Liam Gallagher, I acquired the hair brushed onto the face and the green parka, and I thought a fag hanging out my mouth completed the look.

Whereas other rebels might have chosen the more traditional location of the bike sheds or the school toilets, I found the tennis courts provided the optimum smoking experience. This spot was wide open and right in the middle of the school. The courts were huge, giving you the vantage point that allowed you to see far and wide across the school grounds, like a bird of prey over the African plains, with your predators (the teachers) in your peripheral vision at all times. You could see your predator approaching, their walking pace halted by a restrictive polyester pencil skirt as they'd do that fast-walk-but-still-slow thing towards you, allowing you time to finish your fag in peace. As they got within a few metres of you, you had ample time to have pushed the fag through the fence and then walk away as if nothing had happened: 'Bye Miss!'

Apart from standing around on a tennis court, my only other experience of being near to something called sport was when rollerblading became a thing. I remember that summer well, skating up and down the road, trying to catch the backs of cars for a lift or creating death-defying rollerblading congas attached to the back of someone's BMX down a steep hill. The constant dull ache of a bruised coccyx bone, grazed hands and a scabby chin shaped the summer.

Decades later when I was on the telly hosting something, my dad said, 'You've put on a bit of timber, you should get those rollerblades back out, you've never looked trimmer.' I wasn't 'trim', I was prepubescent.

So there was rollerblading and the fags on the tennis court. But unless that's what Sport Relief had in mind, I wasn't sold.

I couldn't even think why they'd asked me. Did they have some misconception that I was sporty? I had spoken about the footy on air before; maybe they'd heard that and got confused. Maybe they heard I came from a sporting family? Our house was obsessed with Man United, so I was semi-fluent in football. Weekends revolved around Old Trafford: who was picking who up for what game, when they'd be home and what time kick off was. Dad would start Saturday by clapping his hands, big grin on his face, dressing gown blowing as he came down the stairs. 'Keannnnnooooooo,' he'd shout, 'Keannnnnooooooo ... big game today son,' before mimicking the sound of 67,000 United fans in the rafters. As much as I wasn't interested, I did love his excitement; it really got me going too, the ritual of bacon sandwiches and potato cakes for breakfast before layering up for the arctic conditions. Off we'd go to the match. I loved the drive there and the drive back. I loved the bad signal of the AM radio debates about who deserved to win today. I loved the crowds, I loved having a pie, I loved hating the thickness of Bovril but trying to see if I liked it every week, I loved my dad's little shoulder shuffle he did to keep warm as we walked the three miles from the parking to the grounds. I loved everything about it BUT I did not love the actual football. Wow it was boring to me. Each time I went I hoped I'd have a lightbulb moment of clarity where BOOM, I'd get it. Never happened. I'd sit there under duress for the full ninety minutes, feeling like days, as my brain flooded with thoughts . . .

Surely everyone cannot like this?

Why are we outside in December?

Ninety minutes is far too long!

Maybe if I count everybody the time will pass quicker?

These seats aren't comfy, they're too small.

Sorry, what's ACTUALLY going on?

Eventually I'd decide to pluck one question out of my brain and take it to the big man:

'How long's left, Dad?'

'Eighty-four minutes.'

For away games, we'd watch at home and the curtains would be closed, as was tradition, to stop the sunlight blaring through, catching the floating dust hanging in the air. Dad would be in prime position in front of the TV, the carpet worn from where he kicked and stomped his heels during the game as if he were actually playing, and Andrew on the next nearest available sofa. There'd be loud claps and even louder FUCKIN' 'ELLs and SILLY TWATs as my mum would scream back, 'Language, PLEASE!' from the other room. 'It's the bleedin' game!' my dad would argue, and to be fair it was the bleedin' game.

Personally, I respected his passionate swearing, actually impressed by the immense volume he and Andrew could muster from just two human mouths; the house would shake and although I didn't know what they were on about, I loved the drama. As fun as it sounded in there, I'd keep myself anchored to Mum, occasionally being summoned to the lounge by Our Andrew to fetch him a Stella before he asked Dad to remove me for talking. I'd head back next door and perch upon the chrome kitchen stools. I thought the kitchen was cooler anyway than the laddy lounge. I'd sit at the breakfast bar, which I thought was VERY chic, as we blasted Simply Red and the Brand New Heavies as Mum cooked. I'd much rather be in here than the musty football room, I'd think. With the stench of gravy thick in the air, Mum chopped potatoes into chips and sipped on red wine and I'd read our star signs from Mystic Meg. Busy with five pans on the go and a face turned blood-red from the heat of the oven, she'd 'oooh' and 'ahhhh' at the predictions before an ultimate 'Ooh it's a load of rubbish that . . . right, tea's ready!' Perfectly timed to coincide with the football finishing.

And THAT is as close as I got to sport in thirty-five years, hence my apprehension about Sport Relief. Their ask was a little bigger than fetching Stellas for a footy match. The ask was to skate, trek and ski 100 miles in frozen Outer Mongolia and it was the most instant no I've ever given my agent, Caroline, in my life. But after seeing that you can get really nice Mongolian throws, and the price of cashmere out there was rock bottom, I decided to give it a go. You know, for the charity.

Training began one morning on an ice-skating rink in Holloway Road. We were here to master the art of ice skating before applying that, plus cycling and trekking, to a frozen lake for twenty-five miles a day for five days. Before long I was semi-confident about ice skating, having only ever done it drunk at Christmas time and thinking it was all right and a bit of a laugh, surely it would be easy enough to do.

It was here I met my fellow trekkers, for I was not to be alone on this challenge: there was a gang of us, various people off the telly, the news and a pop star assembled as teammates ready to take on this insane challenge, our mission: don't freeze to death, and raise as much money as possible.

We were assigned our balaclavas and puffer jackets, but with a week to go we had an update: due to coronavirus taking over Asia at this time in early 2020, we had to relocate. We'd now be heading to Namibia. Namibia has no ice and, having been to ice-skating training a whole ONE time, I was quite happy with this switch-up. Instead Namibia boasted the world's biggest sand dunes and presented the exact opposite conditions and challenges to what we had been training for. I felt like we'd had a lucky escape – it wouldn't be sub-zero, I might get a tan, sure there'd be no discount cashmere but overall I'd rather be too hot than too cold. Much easier, I thought! Much nicer! It actually will be quite easy!

Cut to me nearly dying on day one. Genuinely.

We land in Namibia and take a helicopter out to the desert. It was a rickety old thing with no sides that looked like it could blow up at any second.

'Don't worry, it's been going for fifty years this chopper,' they said.

Yeah. That's not selling it to me, why is it fifty years old, can't we get a new one? They laughed but I wasn't joking. I piled into the chopper with my co-passengers and trekkers, a hilarious sight for the pilot; there's me, Judge Rinder, Frankie from The Saturdays, Louise Minchin from *BBC Breakfast*, Karim Zeroual from CBBC, Samantha Womack from *EastEnders* and Krishnan Guru-Murthy from the news. Knowing that we could die at any moment, we instantly bonded. Upon landing we excitedly imagined the days ahead around a campfire, with me confidently telling them I'd been to spin class recently in preparation for this and how it can't be harder than spin with a hangover. Can't it?! Oh how wrong I was.

We pair off to settle into our tents for the night, I chose to share with Frankie From The Saturdays so I could learn the dance routines and sing 'Up' to her over and over for a week. Off we go to bed and wake up at the crack of dawn for day one of 100 miles in the desert. It's already hot. Not nice hot like yer holidays hot, hot like when you wake up in a festival hung over and there's no water hot. Or like yer nan's house with a jumper on.

We started and we instantly split up, everyone moving at their own pace. I would have worried about this had I known what was to come, but I felt great. I felt strong, I was figuring out my navigation watch just fine and the sunshine was beating down as I whizzed through this other-planet-like landscape. I had a few hours on my own out there in the middle of nowhere mystified by the space and aura of Africa. I hadn't thought about the magnitude of it all but it was magical, the vastness of it weirdly emotional. Not in a sad way but I began to cry; the simplicity of me versus the land was life-affirming and it was (in a weird way) nice to be forced to think about myself for a few hours – was I drinking enough water, was I going too fast? Had I eaten? It was like an extreme crash course in self-care.

It was also fucking knackering. It was nothing like a spin class with a hangover. It was beyond exhausting, nearing impossible. The heat was excruciating and the bike slow and heavy in the sand. Sometimes it was easier to get off and push it up the dunes, the scalding-hot bike burning your calves as you pushed for your life. I pushed and pushed and fought for every mile of it but it felt like I was going backward. Like in cartoons you see about the desert I could see mirages of the finish line, thinking I was getting closer but only moving minuscule millimetres in the deep thick sand. I began to realise I had underestimated the severity of this challenge.

By 4 p.m. on Monday I'd been out on my bike in 43-degree heat for seven hours, up and down sand dunes, across dry tough desert ground with the wheels barely turning as the hot wind beat my face with such furious heat it felt like when you open the oven while cooking a roast dinner. My face was now blood-red burgundy like my mum's in the kitchen on a Sunday.

Over the course, I'd lost Frankie from The Saturdays and teamed up with Louise Minchin from *BBC Breakfast*, a strong, confident teammate who did mad death-defying challenges like this for fun in her own time. Kindness oozed out of her. She was the perfect wing woman as we cheered each other on and spoke about life, but morale started to fall as we hit some flats. The wind was blowing against us and it was hot, like a hairdryer in your mouth. The sand was almost like gravel here and we were moving at your nan's pace.

A support vehicle drove past, spotted me and pulled me in. I tried to refuse, saying we didn't have long to go to the end and I'd rather just finish, but they insisted. I got off the bike and felt like when you step off the Waltzers – I was still in motion and could barely make the short walk to the car. Everyone looked slightly worried and I couldn't tell if they were just hamming it up for the cameras, but as soon as I sat in the car I started fitting. I was shaking uncontrollably and this deep sense of dark, heavy panic set in. Not the panic you feel when you've lost your keys but full on F E A R. It was instant and the switch from cycling to convulsing was terrifying.

Now I always think I'm dying – of a hangover or from eating an out-of-date vitamin, any time I get on a plane, any time the front door goes. I tend to overdramatise and think death is here to take me away. But as I lay shaking on the back seat of the support car feeling pain all over my body from my face to my toes, my body was no longer my own and I feared I was looking death right in the eyes. I didn't think 'I might die' or 'I feel like I'm dying', I had a feeling that I knew THIS was it. Symptoms aside, I could feel the panic in the air, especially from medics, which is not the greatest thing to experience.

'Am I going to be OK?' I asked through locked jaw and panting shakes.

The response wasn't as instant as I would have liked. It came with a forlorn, saddened face.

'Maybe . . . Just try and breathe and relax,' said the medic.

The thing is, it's not *THAT* relaxing being pulled off a bike by a medical professional in the desert, throwing a fit in the back of a Toyota Land Cruiser as Louise Minchin from *BBC Breakfast* watches open-mouthed and tearful, saying, 'Can you guys do something?'

I saw production members begin to cry and power-smoke fags like detectives about to crack in *CSI: Miami*. Shit I thought, this is it. I was getting worse and one of the doctors, Dr Zoe, told me to think of nice things, to think of my family, and asked me how I'd met my boyfriend and why I loved him so much. I was now freezing cold, full on ugly-sobbing, and as tears rolled down my face and I hyperventilated, and car radios of panicked voices blared from the medic van speakers, I described my love for Meshach to the doctor.

The producers decided to stop. They pulled the day for every-one and we all took the long drive back to camp. I sat clutching on for dear life and I closed my eyes and cried solidly for the three-hour journey, my jaw rattling, teeth chattering and body still flinching from the aftershock. It seemed like the journey took forever, and I worried I'd never feel right again. While my external monologue was just breathy sobs, my internal mono-logue was raging: 'I've ruined this for everyone. It would HAVE to be me wouldn't it, WHY did I do this thing, THIS is why I don't do sport'. The thoughts ran over and over on a continuous loop as we see-sawed up and down the dunes in the 4x4.

We arrive at camp and it's pitch black. Unlike the other camps, on soft sand dunes with a nice view, tonight's camp was beyond creepy. A base filled with dark, withered desert trees, curling around each other, jackals' eyes peering out of them and thick spiderwebs . . . It was giving Addams Family. It was not the ideal environment to experience after you almost died.

Turns out I had extreme heat exhaustion and with my body temperature going up to 40 degrees I'd gone into toxic shock, my body unable to regulate its own temperature.

I hoped when I got back into the tent with Frankie from The Saturdays she'd pop on some of those coloured tights from the 'Up' video and sing me a lullaby and all would be fine. But I wasn't fine, it'd now been seven hours since I stopped the race and I was still going under: 'Why don't I feel better yet?'

I was feeling dark and scared and weak and out of my head. I started seeing things and became paranoid that I was going to be left alone to die. I felt like an extra in *Trainspotting* or something. With no hospital within 200 miles, the doctors were still concerned. The usual jovial camp was silent, in shock as everyone solemnly made up their beds for the night, everyone with a saddened but strong 'Sorry you're about to die in a desert' look on their faces.

FUCKING SPORT RELIEF, I thought. UGH I'm going to die on telly and it's going to look like I've done it for attention. Now I knew I'd be shit at this sport business, but not this shit. I did not expect that at the end of day one – day ONE – I'd be lying on the floor of the Namibian desert surrounded by doctors frantically trying to take my heart readings, cool my 40-degree temperature and inject me with Valium to stop me uncontrollably convulsing. The doctors told me that the desert wasn't designed for such a pasty white person as me.

NO, I KNOW, MY BODY HATES ME, THANK YOU SO MUCH.

They started stabbing my hands in the dark, trying to find a vein. Five milligrams of Valium didn't do it; I was still vibrating, the tent shaking from my twitches. Another ten milligrams injected direct into my hand DID do it, like a light switch. Everything stopped. The silence of the camp was no longer eerie but magical. The desert was no longer my enemy but my lovely warm sandy friend.

I now loved good old sport, lying on the floor, in the dirt, in my underpants, filthy, in a tent, surrounded by strangers. I felt very content. Go sport! I was very grateful to sport now – not only had it taken me on a journey of self-discovery, to the limits of me, taken me to one of the most beautiful places in the world, but it had also introduced me to my one true love: intravenous Valium.

2

Edward

For a long time I grew up carefree. Content and secure. I lived in a gentle suburban setting on the outskirts of Oldham on a horseshoe-shaped family-filled street.

There were two cars on the drive of each house, and in the evenings cordial, chummy chit-chat filled the air as the neighbours watered their hanging baskets flowering with red geraniums.

Mornings were a *Truman Show* chorus of kids and parents waving fond farewells as we set off on our days. Eileen and Pete to work, and me to primary school. I felt safe at school. It was an easy ride, mornings spent making papier mâché while afternoons saw non-competitive PE with little sandbags, or the odd egg and spoon race in the sunshine.

I idled away the day high on Iced Gems, drawing a smiling sun in the corner of every picture my crayons touched. The simplicity of playing, eating and sleeping were the only things crossing my tiny mind – a happy being, content in the comfort of ignorance.

Lol, this sounds so nice!

I was mortgage-free, with no bills to pay and just fucking about with papier mâché! Whereas now I'm a walking, talking blob of anxiety. During those days the only thing that came near to stress was whose turn it was to look after the school gerbils. Bloody loved those gerbils. Like them, I too was living in a fabricated world of cosiness, free from fear of predators, with only the simplicity of playing, eating and sleeping crossing my mind. Hapless beings content in the comfort of ignorance.

Life was cute, and come summertime I spent my days climbing trees in our local park, foraging in the valley behind our house for sticks to throw in the stream or running through nearby fields, Theresa May-style, trying to get the cows to chase me. Should you have a herd of cattle nearby, I'd like to suggest NOT trying this at home. They're faster than you think.

I sported a thick and full bowl haircut and a face filled with freckles, and jaggedy, gappy teeth. I had that childlike confidence; I was fearless, loud and expressive with an unquenchable need for chatter. Summer sang to me, I loved it, it hosted my birthday, it hosted long days for playing out and most of all, it meant no school.

Those summer mornings saw me waking while the cold was still in the air, rushing downstairs for a Pop-Tart, before darting out, coatless and unwashed.

I'd be on a mission, knocking on the doors of my little gang of mates round our way every day. Come rain or shine, we'd be racing our bikes down the steep hills and playing kerby out front until the street lights came on.

It was the summer of 1991, Jazzy Jeff and the Fresh Prince's 'Summertime' was in the air. A summer spent exclusively outside, only stepping foot inside to down a glass of Robinsons Fruit & Barley Cordial from time to time.

'Ahhhhhh . . . that's better. Right, CYA.' I'd bang the glass down on the side before rushing back out.

'Careful! You've spilt that all over the floor! Don't run! Bloody 'ell!' Mum would shout.

'Tea's at six o'clock, you better be back,' she'd call as I sprinted out the back door, leaving it open and tripping over the doormat.

Those six weeks away from school felt like an eternity, the days of scabby knees, dirty hands and ice pops melting in the warm sun stretching on forever. Going back to school after those feral few weeks felt alien. You and your friends morphed into different people – some had shot upwards, some had no teeth, some had new ones, a dodgy cut chin or a skinhead due to a nits outbreak, and jumpers that were too big, were everywhere. But no matter how different we all looked, we were all united in one thing: all unable to remember how to use a pen.

'Oh my God! I can't even write, can you? How mad's that! Pens! OMG, forgot about pens!' The first day, a furore of us repeating that to each other as if we'd been locked in a cave for a decade.

Being forced to look back and analyse the periods of my life for this book, I realised that this summer was the last time I had truly felt carefree. But it was also that summer, when I was seven years old, that my *joie de vivre* came to an abrupt end.

It all happened when I met Edward. Edward changed it all. My summer, my sleep, my life.

Edward, I must explain, is a fictional character. With a very non-fictional effect.

The Edward I'm referring to is one you will know and you may probably even love: the Edward in question is 90s goth icon Edward Scissorhands. A figment of Tim Burton's imagination and the cause of absolute horror in mine. Ughh, even now he gives me the ick.

Edward was introduced to me at the Rochdale Odeon one summer Friday night by my cousin Our Lisa. Like Our Andrew and Our Jane, she was at least a decade older than me, and I LOVED spending time with her. I just thought she was the coolest, up there on my list of adults I idolised. While my siblings had the warrant to tell me 'shut up' and 'goooo away,' Lisa at safe cousin-distance didn't. She took care of me and had this generous energy and a great giggle that used to pop up almost constantly like a hiccup.

She lived round the corner from us with her mum and dad, Auntie Pat and Uncle Dave. I used to love going round as I got full-on attention from another crowd, with my parents no doubt growing increasingly tired of my shows and unreasonable demands to LOOK AT MEEEE.

Pat was my dad's sister, all warm and northern like a good auntie should be, with a brew constantly in hand. She was a great babysitter, taking me to the garden centre for a micro-waved jacket potato on a rainy day or making me cheese and ham sandwiches at hers.

Although older than my parents, they seemed quite mod-ern to me as they had a coffee machine and a black kitchen worktop. They were free from chintz and kept it tidy and simple, not to a Kanye degree of minimalism but on the way there. It was at theirs that I saw my first ever music video, which is etched into my mind as clear as day. I remember sitting cross-legged on their sofa square-eyed at their massive TV and seeing Peter Gabriel throw a salad all over his face for 'Sledgehammer'.

They wore pressed clothes and pruned their immaculate garden daily. While Pat and Dave were a picture of wholesomeness, their daughter, my cousin Lisa, was teetering on the edge of the dark side – think Wednesday from *The Addams Family* with an Oldham accent. She was into metal, the heavier the better. She'd come downstairs with her hair like *The Crow*, in a painted and studded leather jacket, on her way to Rock World on a Monday night. I walked around her bedroom open–mouthed like I was at the Louvre, in awe of the works of art she had acquired. A plastic Pepsi phone, a genuine real-life drumstick and giant posters of Anthrax and Slayer. She blasted Iron Maiden as loud as it would go and I'd jump up and down on her bed screaming as she taught me the lyrics to 'Bring Your Daughter To The Slaughter'.

Lisa took this as a sign that I too was ready for the dark side and ready for the goth-fest of Edward and his scissors. One Friday night, she offered to babysit and spend some quality time with her baby cousin.

Little did we know but it would be a Friday night to change it all. A night that instilled in me absolute fear, pretty much for a lifetime. A night I still think about. A night that Lisa still feels terrible about. To this day she still has second-hand-trauma-giving-guilt because she took me to see stupid Johnny Depp playing a stupid scissor-handed goth. But I don't blame Our Lisa. I blame Eileen and Pete – it clearly states that Edward Scissorhands was a PG – PARENTAL GUIDANCE – they gave no parental guidance! Eileen has still never watched it, claiming, 'It's not scary, it's for kids!'

IT

IS

NOT

FOR

KIDS.

Why they thought I was ready for the horror of *Edward Scissorhands* at age seven is beyond me. It's fucking scary now as an adult, let alone as an actual stupid child with an overactive imagination.

I remember the feel of the cinema that evening. The thrill of the unknown of what was about to happen was in the air, the joy of being out with 'ARLISAAAA' as I pronounced it, without me mum and dad, ran through me. I grew up in a house free of MTV, SKY or any game consoles, so I was chomping at the bit at the idea of watching a movie at 'The Pictures'. We called it that in our house as if it were the actual 1940s, just a slight improvement on calling it 'The Talkies'.

I scoffed down handfuls of popcorn as I wriggled a comfort groove into my seat, spilling the majority down my top and onto the floor as I gazed up in amazement at the big screen. Once the trailers were through and the talking hushed, it began, the movie that would scar me forever. It started in a comfortable, soothing way with a wholesome: 'Once Upon A Time . . .'

A snowy scene appears, a little old lady is telling a bedtime story to her granddaughter. Mmm, this is nice, I thought. It's the story of a young man named Edward. Right, I'm listening.

It's meant to be a sweet story of basic human qualities. One of belonging, of prejudices, of perception and love. It's set in a delightful, seemingly perfect suburban town and begins with us following the life of an Avon rep. She spots a gated mansion that looms over the town and sets off, presumably with the thought that people with mansions love skincare. I smile up at Lisa and settle in as I'm enjoying the looming excitement of where this is going.

The Avon lady breaks into the castle (which seems like such an effort to flog some lippy). If only we had the internet back then cos she could've just done a TikTok at home for Fenty Beauty and been done with it.

It's then we meet the protagonist Edward. He has scissors for hands.

Wait, what.

Scissors for hands?

Is Tim Burton OK hun? The previous six years of my life had been fairy tales and cute cartoons, with the only hard-hitting stuff coming from an edgy episode of *Grange Hill*. Now I was privy to some maniac made by some mad inventor? Fuck this, I thought. Edward is not like the rest of the town, he's an artificial humanoid created by a mad old man in his giant hillside castle. The vision of him will forever be the scariest thing I've ever seen. A burnt-out, battered attic in which we see a figure standing in the moonlight. Hunched over in an outfit The Pussycat Dolls would've loved is Edward. There he is. Peering out with his soulless beady black eyes. SHIT! WHO AND WHAT THE FUCK IS THAT. I grab Lisa's hand and nearly actually shit my pants in the Rochdale Odeon.

He is fucking terrifying.

Rather than finish the job and give him some hands, the mad old man gives him some scissors – why? I know hands are famously hard to draw but are they hard to make? Harder than lungs or a heart? Anyway he can't be fucked making hands, so decides – WHICH IS ABSOLUTELY MENTAL BY THE WAY – to make Edward's hands out of giant gardening blades, hence the punchy nickname. Out of all the utensils to swap hands for, scissors is the worst. Why did he do that? Why not spoons? No hands would be better. All he can do is cut.

Rather than shit her pants and leg it, Avon Lady adopts him – odd decision. Hilarity ensues as Edward tries to fit into this suburban way of life. He starts to give edgy Toni & Guy haircuts to the women around the town. He's a sweet, confused man who's been neglected and now is in search of love and human connection. He's a good egg with a sweet soul longing for acceptance and a place in this world.

Everyone cheered him on and wanted him to be loved but I fucking hated him. He didn't just give me a little bit of the ick, I could vomit. I hated his look. Robert Smith on Atkins. Seeing him gave me a full physical body convulsion, like swallowing down a bushtucker trial. The deep baggy purple bags under his eyes, the bewildered, lost look across his face. Ew. It's even sending me under now. The erratic haunting hair, jet black and stood on end, against the hallowed white skin, covered in new thick blood-red scars over raised old pink ones on their way to recovery. He moved erratically like a spider; you never knew which way he was going to go. I couldn't read him.

I didn't realise it at the time but those few hours of sitting and being quiet in the Rochdale Odeon, well, they fucked me up. I remember standing up and walking across the crunchy, pop-corn-strewn carpet in silence. Ever since then, in similar scenes, with every single hangover I've ever had I have been spooked and scared by anyone and anything.

'Wahhhh!' I'd scream and jump out of my skin at a car turn-ing its lights on.

'HOLY . . .!' at a man firing up his motorbike.

This was the first time I'd experienced any other emotion than just loveliness. What the fuck was going on? As we walked across the car park, I looked up at Our Lisa for reassurance, which didn't help. With her black hair, pale skin, leather jacket – I had to check that she wasn't concealing secateurs for fingers.

'Awwwww I loved that, did you?' Our Lisa asked.

I was shell-shocked. 'Erm . . . yeh. Yeh, loved it.'

But no Lisa, I didn't, I absolutely did not love it.

I got home way past my regular bedtime and for the first time in my seven years of breathing, I was quiet.

'He must be tired,' Eileen said as I was commanded upstairs to bed.

I looked up at the stairs and felt uneasy. I felt The Fear. Me? Upstairs? Alone? Upstairs near the attic? Like the one Edward lives in? Fuuuuuuck that . . . I made it halfway before running back down into the lounge.

'Get up the bleedin' stairs!' Pete said, 'and get to bleedin' sleep.'

Eileen walked me up and I gripped her hand like a vice, each step creating miles of distance between the adults together downstairs and me alone in the dark upstairs. The floral carpet and the dark looming shadows of the bannisters reminded me of the movie I'd just watched.

'Please can I have a lamp on?' I asked.

Mum reassured me that everything was fine and a movie star from Hollywood with scissors for hands was NOT going to get me. I made her check my wardrobe. He wasn't in there. I made her check behind the curtains. He wasn't there either.

'OK?' she asked, 'now get to sleep!'

It was a time before we could pause TV, and she was missing *Band Of Gold*.

She went down and I lay there in dead silence, my body rigid, scared to move in case Edward could sense my motion. I was boiling hot, the prang-out causing my body to heat up to ungodly temperatures and sweat through my blue polyester Transformer pyjamas. I tried to breathe quietly and kept my eyes as wide open as possible. Every creak, every raindrop, every slight groan of the house made me throw the duvet up in the air, high-jump out of the bed and fly down the stairs into the living room.

One lamp wasn't cutting it, I needed another. Then the big light, then the landing light, until at night every single light would be on upstairs. 'It's like bleedin' Blackpool illuminations up 'ere!' Pete would say before flicking off the landing light, to my banshee wailings.

'ARRRRGGGHHHHHHHHHHHHHH! He's gonna get me! IT'S TOO SCARY UP THERE!'

'He is NOT going to get you!' Pete would shout up.

'HE IS! I KNOW IT! HOW DO YOU KNOW HE'S NOT?' I'd holler back, my voice trembling with fear.

'Because he's not bleedin' real. Now get to bleedin' sleep will ya? Bleedin' soft lad.' Pete was rightly over this nightly carry-on.

I'd creep out of my room and onto the landing. We had this big oblong window that stretched over the stairs across the front of the house, giving a wide-lens view over our suburban street. Oh shit, it looked like the movie. The bungalows, the hanging baskets, the driveways. It looked like the perfect place for Edward. I'd have visions of him walking down the street, his PVC bodysuit wet in the Mancunian rain and glimmering in the street lights. I started to have actual hallucinations, convinced that I had seen him (I obvs hadn't). They became part of my nightly routine. Normal.

It cast an Edward-shaped shadow over my life. I thought about bedtime all day, I dreaded it, I rode my bike home faster, I made sure I was home before the street lights flickered on, and spent more time inside. The bright days were fine, but cloudy dark days and the fall of dusk triggered my impending sense of doom. I started to look over my shoulder when I was out in the street. And now at this grand old age, I still do: the lasting effect of Edward.

Still to this day I get asked by laughing aunties, 'You're not still scared of that Edward fella are ya? Haha, ooooooh you didn't sleep for years!'

My response is: yes actually I am still scared of Edward actually. Like a first love, I just can never forget him. He was like a very scary marinade in my brain; I just couldn't shake him off. Cry as I might and try as they might, there was nothing anyone could say or do to help with my crisis. I was a night-time nervous wreck.

I served a long stint under the cruel eye of Edward fear and before long it felt normal. It was just what bedtime was about. Not rest but hours of exhausting panic before my body finally collapsed from not-enough-hours' sleep. It legitimately conditioned me to be like this. I got used to fearing bedtime. Sunsets gave me a shudder, not full of romantic colours for me but a big scary sign that it would be dark soon. And when it was dark, helloooooo anxiety! Like *his* fucked-up face, I was scarred and damaged and in desperate need of a medical professional to repair me. This went on for weeks. Then months. Then years.

I don't remember getting over it cos I don't think I ever did. My Edward fear merely mutated away from his scissor-handed self and into just being scared of anything, everything and everyone. It evolved into this prang of being attacked and killed in bed so I'd be scared to sleep even as a fully functional adult. As something of a night owl, it was a bloody nightmare for me. Figuratively and literally. I'd happily host my evening radio show in the safe basement of the old Radio 1, then shit my pants rushing to my car, holding my keys between my knuckles, before jumping in and locking the doors at break-neck speed. I'd check the back seats to make sure my murderer wasn't lurking back there to get me from behind. Some nights I'd work myself up so much that I'd have to get out of bed and drive over to stay at friends' houses. I was no longer seven years old, I was twenty-five, twenty-eight, even thirty-one. I'd happily choose an uncomfortable night's sleep on a friendly sofa over my own luxurious bed if it meant I didn't have to be alone. I was told by a friend that this was very narcissistic. The belief that someone should want to make the effort to murder me in my own home in the middle of the night was an unrealistic fear. 'They'd just run you over if they wanted to.' True. But I could never shake it.

I only spoke to my therapist about it years later. Once we'd done trauma, mourning, gay guilt, regular guilt and Catholic guilt we got onto the easy breezy 'Oh yeah, btw forgot to mention, I'm absolutely terrified of being alone.'

I told her how now, when I watch things they stay with me. And I'm dragged back to being that seven-year-old kid in my single bed. I watched *Luther* and had to go stay at a friend's house. I'd watch *Silent Witness* and have to do a YouTube deep-breathing tutorial. It used to just be horrors or murder documentaries but it's now spilled out into the anxiety-inducing genre too – *Euphoria* – too trippy, forget it. Even a particularly icky social interaction on *The Office* can send me under.

I told her how I dream of the horrors of these shows, they disrupt my sleep and cloud my mind with eerie thoughts that stilt my productivity and elbow my own happiness out of my head. I needed a solution from her. I told her that I feel the fear in a scary programme as much as the character. I told her that if I watch a show and someone is being chased I feel like I'm being chased. If they're being murdered, I feel like I'm getting murdered. I said scary stuff is too scary for me. Her solution was groundbreaking.

'Don't watch them then,' she said.

'Oh yeah! Hadn't thought of that.' Genuinely. I gave her fifty quid and left, revelling in her breakthrough professional suggestion. Just don't watch them then. So I don't. I refuse to watch anything slightly triggering now. I'm on a strict diet of Attenborough. It drives Mesh mad but I try to spin it, to see it as a good thing. Just avoiding drama, maybe it's a good attribute for real life? Yeh maybe. Or maybe it's just ruined us watching anything good on Netflix.

When I was a kid, I suggested we fly to LA to meet Johnny Depp. Then years later I went to meet actual Edward Scissorhands, Mr Johnny Depp, at his hotel. I was there to interview him about his new movie but I also saw this as a mental health workshop. I was supposed to ask about his movie *The Lone Ranger* but decided to tell him immediately why I was REALLY there. 'I was shit-scared of you as a kid.' Then I couldn't shut up about it, reeling out every symptom, issue and my mother's concerns. I look at the PR, who is urging me to ask Johnny about the movie that he made this year, not the one he made twenty-three years ago. Fair. I ask him about his horse on set and all I can do is stare in his beady Edward eyes and start to sweat. It was probably the worst interview of my life, mainly cos I wasn't listening to a word he said, I was just trying to suppress the internalised horror as I saw the Edward jump out of him.

I bring it up one more time, as I don't think he understands the severity of it. He tells me, 'I'm sorry for scaring you as a child.' I accept his apology and tell him I'm over it now . . . I'm not but it's nice to be nice isn't it. Not saying that he was scary but the usual three minutes, which normally is never enough, felt like hours and I was happy to flee for a calming emergency alcoholic beverage.

Then last Christmas, something magical happened. We were forcibly locked in the house with a festive Covid infection and I was flicking through the channels, on my seventh hour of TV for the day. 4 p.m. Channel 4. *Edward Scissorhands*. The Covid was for sure fucking with my brain because I decided I would watch it. I settled in with my obligatory December cheese and biscuits and decided to finally face my fears. I started to feel hot and panicked but then something happened . . .

Was I *actually* scared of Edward Scissorhands??? Or did my childhood fear stem from being scared of the fact that I was actually into homosexual BDSM goth fetish looks?

Cos watching now, Edward Scissorhands is hot. Like, really hot. Like, screaming on your sofa, howling at the moon, calling-your-friends-to-tell-them HOT. I mean he's a complex, artistic, misunderstood man with a giant hillside mansion overlooking the city. He's a mysterious, sexy outsider who can give you a short back and sides from time to time. What's not to love?

As the film plodded on, I got it. I finally saw what Our Lisa saw. The softness of Edward. He wasn't trying to kill me. He was trying to show me it's OK to be an Edward. He was showing me it's OK to be different and actually, maybe all the perfect people judging Edward are the fucked-up ones. I'd spent a lot of time feeling like the odd one out. Growing up, I worried how my suburban life would look – with no wife and no kids. I realised my gayness was my point of difference. It's not scissors for hands but both of us had these THINGS that made us feel different.

I was Edward. His social awkwardness that I experienced in my teenage years was like looking in a mirror. Not literally, cos as aforementioned, he was undeniably hot. But you know what I mean. The rest of the town led a life I never wanted – they went to work and went home. They wore perfectly fine clothes that matched their perfect houses. Their lives a perfect postcard picture of heterosexuality. I saw now that I wasn't like the other residents, fearing Edward. I *was* Edward, my gayness creating feelings of non-conformity, and I increasingly felt like an outsider. While I wasn't walking around in a black all-in-one catsuit, I started to recognise some of me in Edward. I was a weirdo too. Not THAT weird but still weird enough. He couldn't conform and I also couldn't conform to the other boys at school with their Rockports and Helly Hansens – the schoolboy look *du jour*. I wanted to wear my mum's white Burberry trench to school with buckled shoes from Russell & Bromley and a blue plastic ring I'd got in a cracker. But while I loved the white trench, the others did not.

'You look like you work in the freezers at ASDA,' they laughed. They had a point.

I never thought I'd watch this movie again, forever scared by the fear of this creepy outsider. I now realised not only that I was Edward. I also realised that semi-pissed, fully snotty Covid-strewn day that over my life I have craved Edwards. Picking the outsiders, the oddballs, the interesting ones, the hot ones? I realised it's not a scary movie at all but a tale of understanding and acceptance, of not judging a book by its cover – just cos he's in a PVC catsuit doesn't mean he's a meanie. Let the man live!

We both went on journeys, we both felt like outsiders, we both felt the need to conform and we both were massive fans of Winona Ryder.

I don't know if it was the Covid or the wine or the Covid-drenched wine but I was left feeling comforted and seen. When the film finished, I ran to tell Mesh in the kitchen: 'MESH! I'm Edward Scissorhands! He's not bad! Neither am I! I mean what even is good and what is bad? What is normal? Is anyone normal?! WOW! I'm him! That's why I was so obsessed with him!'

Mesh looked like he wanted to leave me. I smiled and headed upstairs as I exhaled out my Edward horror for the first time in thirty-one years. My one true gut-wrenching horror had become my greatest teacher. That night, I lay in the dark in peace and wished myself, and Edward, a sound night's sleep. Us weirdos have to look out for each other.

3

Leather Gloves and Toast

There's a lot about my life that I don't know. I don't know my first word, where I took my first steps or what time of day I was born. I'd never really thought to ask about these ancient memories. Are they even my memories to have? I know I was a wriggly baby in the womb who was so rambunctious in there that Eileen was forced to have an emergency C-section as I refused to keep still. But that's about it. Writing this book made me sit and think back across all aspects of my life, and some are just black spaces, spanning years – some due to copious amounts of alcohol and some due to my tiny, infantile brain. I started thinking about school before trying to go back further and further each time. I'd never really thought about my very first memory before. The first time that I screenshotted some life and filed it away forever. I had to rack my brains til my eyes hurt to try to pinpoint my first burning memory. I find it. It's not great. I remember finding myself strapped in a car seat in an empty car. I was so small that I could just about stretch up to see a millimetre or so of sky from the bottom of the window. I remember crying and being collected out of the seat and taken to see Gran Nora, Eileen's mum, in her flat. I remember stopping crying and seeing the fruit and veg market of Rusholme through tear-stained eyes, as Eileen dodged traffic with me in her arms. Gran Nora had a floral, scratchy sofa that I clawed at with my nails. I remember her thin skin feeling cold and her hair the texture of candyfloss in a hot, toxic, Ziggy Stardust shade of orange. The memory is so blurry that I worry I'm remembering a dream, one art-directed by myself after looking at old family pictures of Nora smoking away in her armchair. I decided to call Eileen to check that I had actually been and she tells me we used to go weekly, with Nora saying my birth was the lease of life she needed at her grand age.

While that memory was blurred and trippy, my next formative early memory was one I didn't have to search for. It was one I still smile to myself about today, should I get a waft of toast.

I always remember the mornings, for some reason. I remember the feel of the blur of morning TV, of the hairsprayed omnipresent smiles of weather girls and bright-coloured pencil-skirt suits. I'd slurp up my Coco Pops as the smell of burnt toast filled the house and set the smoke alarm off. Eileen would flap a tea towel around with a flushed face, then run outside, letting all the cold in, to defrost the car. I'd watch from the window as she scraped the ice off her blue Ford Fiesta with the new scraper she'd bought from a catalogue. I don't know if it was my fault or Mum's fault but we were always running late for school and tensions were often high. We followed a strict daily ritual, always late and never on time but sticking to the routine.

With breakfast now over, she'd jump in and fire up the motor. The engine would chug along as fumes billowed out the back and the mild hum of chatter from the radio inside the car began. It felt like winter was never-ending and we spent most days fighting the frost. I'd see her head pop out and she'd wave like a woman in distress, both arms overhead, to signal it was time to leave. I'd run to the driveway, meeting the car face on, and I'd have to squeeze round between the front of the car and the garage door. Standing in front of a car was always a nauseating prospect; the threat of immediate death from being crushed was a daily fear. Especially when the car was revving along with no driver at the control, the driver instead frantically trying to de-ice it like a mad scientist on a cryogenics course.

I am instructed to get in and wind the windows down, the ice so thick and solid on the glass that winding down the handle requires all of my four-year-old muscles and determination. The handle to do the window won't budge. The doors feel hollow like they could buckle in your hands, the ice becoming glue: 'It won't go down!' I shriek with the intensity of the captain on the *Titanic*: 'The ice, it's too much!'

'That's fine love, don't worry.' Eileen has an air of panic. She looks eagerly through the face-sized porthole she's managed to scrape out of the frost. 'That'll have to do or we're gonna be late,' she says with worry, looking at me, aged four, for reassurance. 'Yehhh you can see out . . . a bit,' she says.

She gets in alongside me and I watch her pop on her black leather driving gloves. A glove exclusively saved for driving her Fiesta round Royton. She's foot to the floor, revving the Fiesta like Lewis Hamilton at Silverstone. I'd like to say she mastered it but to THIS day my mother cannot get her car off the drive. Our front drive was on a downwards slope that you drove into and reversed up, and as a child it loomed like Everest, a death-defying climb up to the top. I'd think getting a car on there would be a stunt even Tom Cruise himself would decline. In reality, looking at it as an adult, it's about a 10-degree angle and about one average hatchback in length.

With the fumes-a-flowing and the Fiesta almost doing a handstand it sounds like we're about to take off, here we go, the moment of truth ... VVVVVRRRROOOMMMMMMNNNNNNN. Eileen's leather driving gloves are gripping the wheel for dear life. She huffs with the crazed look of Cruella de Vil in her eyes. Her nemesis the driveway is NOT going to win today. NO SIR! HERE WE GO! COME ON MOTHER, YOU'VE GOT THIS, I think as I grip the hollow cold sides of the car and hope for the best. She removes one hand and lowers it down, shaking in anticipation like she's about to defuse a bomb, and grips the handbrake, thumb over the click-in button. She presses the button. It feels like it's going in slow motion and that's because it IS going in slow motion. I've seen space expeditions take off quicker. Once she's checked the mirrors for the fourth time, NASA are informed and she begins to lower the handbrake, foot pressed so hard into the clutch it causes her varicose veins to flare. Away we go! Is today going to be the day that we take off to school first time?? No. No it is not. She smacks the wheel with a muted 'Fucksake!' Fail. The Fiesta, like us, falls silent in defeat. It feels sad in here now. With the ice still clogging the windows it's hard to see if a crowd has formed to boo and hiss, but it certainly feels that way. We go again. DING DING, round two, Eileen in the red corner, starting to cling to the ropes a little, and the undefeated Mount Kilimanjaro of suburbia in the blue corner.

As the fury of 'This bloody drive! I told Pete I hated this bloody drive!' starts to pour out of Mum, the frost starts to thin and I can start to see out of it. We had a big long unconventional window along the front of the house and up in it is a mysterious winter figure. What is that I see on this cold winter morning? Santa? Oh no, it's my father, in his dressing gown, who is very animatedly gesturing and trying to mouth something to us. Maybe he's here to offer support – well, he is raising his hands in the air. I lower the window frame and the now-softened ice is more a slush as it flops off, half onto my knee. I try to focus on what he's saying. I can't work out exactly what it is but a lot of the words start with F.

'Mum, I think Dad wants you . . .'

He opens the window and hangs half out, his floppy gown blowing in the cool morning breeze.

'Oh piss off!' she says, shaking her thick Tina Turner-like hair and resettling herself. She fires up the mum-mobile, the radio starts and The Clash are playing 'Should I Stay Or Should I Go'. It may as well have been 'Eye Of The Tiger', as THIS time she means business. Her steely determination fixated on the dash, she goes through the motions – mirror, clutch, handbrake, let's do this! She hits the pedal and as all of Ford's engineering prowess is put to the test she releases the handbrake and we begin to move. Forward. She slams on the brakes inches from next door's brick wall, which juts out into ours. Oh boy. There was a feeling growing up, presumably created from my parents' hard-working mentality, that should anyone scratch the car, the world would implode and everyone would die. Years later when I learnt to drive, I adopted the more obnoxious 'Well that's what insurance is for' outlook, which drove Pete mad.

Now, with Pete's eyes upon her, Eileen has something to prove. If this were a movie 'R-E-S-P-E-C-T' by Aretha would start playing as my mother fires up the 1.1 litre engine to the max. Attempt number three and we shoot off the drive and down the road to school leaving those pesky men (well, my dad) in the dust! YEH GIRL POWER! I am slightly concerned that I am in the hands of a woman who's just taken ten minutes to get off her own driveway and is now loose on the icy roads with a windscreen still semi-opaque from frost and the steam permeating from her own ears, but I have faith and turn up the radio.

We sped up the main drag just off our road, a wide road full of the posh houses that led onto a leafy park. On cold snowy days like today, the road would always be filled with dog walkers with their dogs in little fluffy jackets, and happy folk carrying their sledges for a day of frolicking in the snow. A total Christmas-card scene. 'They should put bloody gates on this road and charge people,' my dad used to say, 'bloody everyone here using the road and the park,' the road he doesn't live on and the park he's rarely ventured into, that is.

From there we descended into Royton, our local town, park-ing at the precinct opposite my nursery. It was a large red-brick building below a modern church we didn't go to and next to a mammoth Chinese restaurant of the same biblical scale and even more than its religious neighbours' sense of grandiose.

It's here we met Eileen's other daily nemesis. Now she was OUT of the drive, she had to contend with getting IN to a parking space. I won't relay the ins and many, many outs of this attempt to park, as this book only has 70,000 words but it was never exactly a three-point turn. Thirty-three maybe. I jumped out of the car and was hurried across the car park. Eileen's leather driving gloves now removed, she grabbed my hand to cross the road, down the nursery stairs, and noticed my hand temperature: 'Ooooh, your hands are like toast! Have a great day! See you at three!' She kissed me and turned back up the stairs to head to work.

I was stuck staring at my hands. What was meant as a passing comment on noticing my cosy toddler hands threw me into a hole. I wasn't nuanced enough in the 'toast is a cosy byword for warmth' thing, so my head imploded. Toast? My hands? Are LIKE TOAST? What on earth did she mean? Edible? Crispy? Delicious? Burnt? Should I taste them? Was someone going to try and eat them today? I thought I better hide them as quickly as possible, shoving them into my pockets as the nursery assistant fought to get my coat off.

'Lift yer 'ands out, Nick,' she said.

She's trying to eat my hands, I thought as I wriggled them further away from her clutches in a bid to keep my hands intact. 'Nooooooooo,' I screamed as Eileen reached the top of the stairs. 'I'll be back at three, don't cry!' she said.

'But my handssss . . .' She couldn't hear me, she was gone. I couldn't believe she had just left me like that to fend for my bread-like hands. I was left with a whole day thinking WHY my hands were like toast.

The clock struck three and after an anxiety-filled day of trying to decipher Mother's ludicrous mind-boggling statement – TOAST LIKE MAD BREAD HANDS – I saw her approaching, threw down my Lego and screamed, 'MUM MUM MUM WHY ARE MY HANDS LIKE TOAST?'

'Eh? Toast?' she asked.

'YES YES YES TOAST! YOU SAID MY HANDS ARE LIKE TOAST ARE THEY GONNA GET EATEN?!'

'What yer on about? Get yer coat— ohhh cos they were warm . . . warm like toast!' She burst out laughing remembering her morning comments and seeing the look of dread and panic in my eyes. Excuuuuse meee . . . Not very funny, I thought as we walked back to the car for no doubt another *Top Gear*-level adventure out the car park. We got home and Eileen made me toast and I checked the temperature of the grilled bread against the backs of my hands. Her morning point was valid.

As we got closer to home, Eileen cracked up again, her giggles becoming infectious and I raised my hands to the windscreen and laughed along, imagining them covered in butter. I guess your first memories do matter, I guess they do shape you. My very first solid memory, which set the course for the rest of my life, the things that would go on to define me: Eileen, Pete, being late, anxiety and delicious, warm, friendly carbohydrates.

4

Fat Boy Roy

My dad had a massive head. Logan Roy of *Succession* big. It looked heavy and powerful, all knowing and seasoned with age. As a child it looked huge to me, and even when he died I marvelled at the size of his almighty skull. You hear about men's ears growing with age, but my dad bucked the trend and invited the rest of his face along for the ride; the head was large and in charge, a hat-maker's nightmare.

Pete was born in 1941 in Manchester. 'I was a war baby,' he used to say as he reminded us of having fuck-all and eating 'drippin' butties,' a hearty meal of lard sandwiched between chunky white bread slices. Yet to try but it's on my to-do list once I've finished this book. He liked the simple, hearty meals that a proper northerner should: egg and chips, 'tata-ash' and occasionally he'd opt for the 'healthy' brekkie option and would chow down on croissants laden with inches of butter and jam, arguing with us that it was healthy as it was 'bleedin' continental!'

Food was important in our house; we'd be asking what's for tea when we were still chewing our brekkies down. We were celebrated by cousins for our always-stacked biscuit tin, full of Viscounts and Clubs and Mum's sad WeightWatchers ones that no one wanted. It lived in the cupboard by the cooker alongside multipacks of crisps and packs of malt loaf. The other side of the cooker was a cupboard dedicated to bread. Just bread. Everyone had their own specific bread demand. Our Jane liked Toastie Loaf, Eileen had to have a Hovis and Pete liked proper bread from the bakers that you'd have to slice yourself, covering the entire kitchen in a crusty confetti. I wanted Milk Roll, which was made in Blackpool and came in these mini round batches. It was mouldable in your hands and I'd squeeze it tightly to get my fingers printed into it like a movie star on Hollywood Boulevard. Heaven forbid that we should run out of bread. And when we frequently did, scenes in our kitchen were like that of a submarine under attack in a war film, red lights flashing, sirens, men taking their own lives. A slight exaggeration maybe, but not far off.

Pete worked in sales for Findus (and its parent company), travelling around the country flogging vinegar, coffee, chocolate, frozen meals and everything in between. He worked hard and long hours but it was well worth it cos he used to get to bring home loads of battered products. We were snowed under by deranged KitKats that were deemed unsellable. They were the outcasts, the freaks of the confectionery world, made with a fifth finger, or the machine had gone crazy and forgotten the wafer, rendering them solid and waferless. From time to time we'd get some nearly-out-of-date Nesquik – a personal afterschool essential of mine – tins of Carnation milk or the odd, always vile but willing to try every time, Walnut Whip.

We'd stuff our faces with a smorgasbord of faulty Findus products from the boot of Dad's white Rover. Once, complaining about KitKat monotony and that they were a bit boring, I was made privy to the well-rehearsed choccy propaganda etched into Pete's brain: 'We sell six KitKats a second the world over, I'll have you know!' Sorry, all respect to my dad and Findus for putting a roof over our heads, but who the fuck chooses to buy a KitKat?

Some families have mantras or sentiments they live by. We didn't but if we did it would be 'WHAT'S FOR TEA?' Jane, Andrew, me and Pete all wailing it round the house. Weekends saw Eileen cheffing it up in the kitchen, whipping up the best roast dinner I've still ever had to this day, ten pans going all at once, but weekday nights the answer to the eternal question of what's-for-tea was a lot less cheffy: 'Whatever's in the freezer!' We had one of those coffin-like freezers in the garage, long, white and humming along, stuffed to the brim with Findus products. I'd squeeze through the always-broken stupid door into the garage and step onto the cold floor, carefully dodging Pete's company car and spiders' webs for a glimpse into the icy grotto of dreams . . . mmmmm crispy pancakes, French bread pizza and boil-in-the-bag curries from Lean Cuisine. Ideally I'd opt for the French bread pizza, as the words 'pizza' and 'French' seemed positively futuristic in a house ruled by people born in the 1940s. I loved them and felt that they were the height of the modern culinary world. For afters we could have one of the faulty KitKats, washed down with a Perrier water with the label on upside down. My brother still claims to this day that the reason he is bald is his exclusively frozen-food diet of the 1970s and 80s.

Once tea was done it was time to delay bedtime. I'd have a mooch around Mum and Dad's room where Eileen used to keep all family photos in the drawers under her bed – not on show, hung up or placed in an album but shoved in a drawer never to be seen again. It drove me and Our Jane mad.

'I haven't got time! I'll frame them next week!' Eileen would protest. Still hasn't.

Plastic bags of photos were hidden away like a famous family heirloom, only to be discovered when Our Jane and I had sunk to such depths of boredom we would get them out – 'Make sure you put them all back,' Eileen would yell; 'Well there's no point having them if we can't look at them!' we'd reply.

Whipping past all the ones we'd seen of us as babies, 80s trips to Texas to visit Uncle Mike, and a beehived Eileen at a 'dance' in 'town', we found Pete's school photos. Aged, in actual sepia like the joke Western ones you'd have at Alton Towers. There he was sat in the middle of rows of schoolboys at Corpus Christi Roman Catholic School. He must have been eight. He looked forty. 'Look at the size of his head! He had the same sized head then!' Jane and I fell about in hysterics as we showed my mum, who burst out laughing, pissing herself too for a good minute before composing herself and saying, 'Ahhhhh don't be mean. Don't laugh at him.'

I presumed it had grown bigger and bigger over the decades but looking back at these pictures it was a wonder to behold even back then. Pete hadn't grown this big head as he grew himself, he was born with this giant wonder of the science world. It wasn't just the size of his head, his face looked exactly the same too. Same haircut, same smile and same calm big camel eyes. He actually looked better post-forty; he kept looking eternally forty. As someone who has inherited much of my dad in terms of mannerisms and big nose, I'm hoping this is what happens to me too. I hope that the looking-forty-forever thing works for me and I become the real life Benjamin Button.

Like Pete, I too was born with a big fat head. Apologies to Eileen and her pelvis but my day one baby pictures look like she gave birth to a chunky toddler, not a newborn. Thick hair, wrists and ankles so swollen that I made the Cabbage Patch Dolls look svelte. Most babies have a dainty fragile little sweet skull that you 'must support'. Mine looked like it was ready to take a round with Tyson Fury.

So we had the same head and ye-olde-looking face, but the place where we differed was everything from the head down. As we looked back at old pictures and the man I knew as a soft-round-the-edges, golf-playing, bread-loving, classic DADBOD owner was an absolute bloody racehorse of a man! HANG THE FUCK ON – what? Why is his body like that? It was ripped. And I mean Hollywood movie star ripped. Pete's bod back in the day was giving Brad Pitt in *Fight Club*. I was shocked. Partly because I didn't recognise this guy in the pictures – he's not what MY dad looks like – and mainly because, where was my inherited Brad Pitt bod? What the fuck! I got all the rubbish bits! His gappy teeth yes, his large head yes, his impatience yes! Six-pack and shoulders carved from marble? No.

Being the youngest one, not brought into the world until Pete was forty-three, by the time I was going through puberty and thinking about my body, Pete was well into his fifties. I had missed the glory days of Pete's six-pack and in hindsight I'm happy I did, because no one wants unrealistic body goals that close to home when they're a flabby teenager. I'm happy that I got the soft edges of Pete's frame and didn't grow up feeling like Kaia Gerber looking across the kitchen at Cindy Crawford. When I was a kid I knew he loved football, but I didn't realise until I was older that he used to love all exercise – running, squash, football, sometimes all three in a day. He'd run to squash, play for an hour, then run home or run laps of our local park till he hit marathon miles. Hence the bod. I did not have this same passion for sweating. Hence the bod.

Once I hit my teenage years my dad tried politely to help me lose the puppy fat I'd acquired over years of orange Club biscuit abuse and form a bond over sport. Try as he might to inspire me and include me, sport was not to be the vehicle required to solidify our bond. He tried it all. There was the cross-country running; I'd run across a muddy field, complaining the entire way round. He'd collect me in the car, me shivering and nearly crying: 'I came eighteenth,' I'd say and he'd say, 'It's the taking part that counts.' Well, no, not in a race it isn't, but whatever. Football he did not even try with after he saw my 'skills' in the street with the other kids. He said my legs were a waste of good footballing legs as I tippy-toed around the lounge pretending to be Cilla Black.

'What about golf?' he asked, the last chance saloon at bonding over something vaguely alpha. Maybe THIS sport would inspire me to go outside. I will say the pace of golf appealed to me more,

I liked that you got to wear a fun outfit, it was non-contact and it was free from my peers. Everyone there was a more forgiving target audience: all were at least sixty. I trusted the sixty-year-olds more; they weren't trying to suss me out or judge my campness, and we shared the same love for a nice biscuit and a passion for *The Royal Variety Performance*. 'Let's give it a go, maybe golf will be my thing,' I thought.

We arrived at the golf club one clear day and Pete told me that, after I showed the vaguest glimpse of interest in his clubs in the garage, he had bought me a block of lessons. I remember using the wooden-looking blobby one as a microphone, just like I'm sure all golfers do in their dad's garage. That morning felt serene, like the dawn of a new day, as we looked out over the vast landscape of the manicured course and into our future as a golfing double act. Father–son activity here we go. We'd be sport's Stavros Flatley. I was instructed to stand like this, hold my hands like this, my back like this, my eyes look here, my arms go there . . . I didn't like it. 'Wait, this is too strict,' I complained, 'can't I just hit it?'

'YOU HAVE TO FOLLOW THE RULES!' Pete bellowed. After a short squabble, I was frogmarched back to the car, clubs plonked in the boot and doors slammed: 'bleeeedin' waste of bleeeeedin' time.' My golfing career was over. So were my father's attempts at making me into a sportsman.

Sport at school was even worse. It still makes my anxiety flare up thinking about it. I HATED IT: hockey was cruel, the competitiveness of football hell on earth and rugby near-torturous.

On a dog walk, even now, the smell of wet mud can still throw me back to PE where we'd attempt rugby on the back field, an absolute free-for-all that resulted in bruises, black eyes and frostbite. My PE teacher was strict but bouncy, genuinely enjoying the sports, rounding everyone up, jogging ahead and throwing balls around. Sorry but it's cold AND wet, why would we do this? It defied logic to me; I just didn't get it and would protest its place in the syllabus weekly. Whereas with history or English I could sit and daydream out the window, with a vague interest in learning something about something, this was the only lesson that wasn't a lesson. It was expected that I arrive and just know how to play rugby. I wouldn't turn up to IT and be expected to know how to programme a computer; it would take months of learning, so why is PE this unregulated *Hunger Games*? The only thing I knew about rugby was that there was a player called a 'hooker', and that made me think of Julia Roberts. And the second thing I knew about rugby was: don't try that little Julia Roberts gag with your rugby teacher.

Off we'd go onto the pitch, mud frozen solid and the air biting from the dark grey sky turning my legs bright pink and bumpy. The ones who knew how to play grabbed the ball and ran forward as others chased and tackled them to the ground. 'Get involved, Grimshaw!' the PE teacher would shout. Not being funny but absolutely not a chance. I'd kill time during the match avoiding the ball, feigning a stitch, pretending I was running full speed but just couldn't keep up and encouraging others to go after it instead – 'That's yours, you've got this!' I'd say things I didn't understand like 'Good ball!' and 'Well in!'

but I knew it wasn't for me, I knew at this young age I just didn't have the hardness required to want to chase, grab and wrestle a man to the floor for a pleather ball. There were some others who I knew felt the same – the short ones, the skinny ones, the goth ones, we were the last picked, the outsiders, and easily spotted as we were mud-free and avoiding eye contact.

'Why's there no mud on you, Grimshaw?' the rugby dictator asked once. I was unable to muster up a good enough response and he gave me some absolutely insane directions: 'Drop ont' floor and roll in that puddle.'

DROP

ON

THE

FLOOR

AND

ROLL

IN

THAT

PUDDLE.

What a fucking joke, I thought, I'll tell him to do one, I thought. Instead I dropped to my knees, feeling a wet splash of mud up my legs, and flopped onto my side, where I rolled in a muddy puddle to satisfy the need of my PE teacher, hell-bent on making me not inspired but just a bit wet. Once he was satisfied with the muddiness I was allowed up and into the changing rooms, the room thick with BO that everyone attempt-ed to mask with Lynx Africa. Not reading the seriousness of the male changing room after a volatile game of rugby, I clearly remember trying to start a conversation: 'Omgggg did you see the Spice Girls at the Brits last night? I feel like I know that song so well already, it's got to be a cover, right?' before singing the killer hook of the chorus. Silence.

My lack of sporting prowess and my inability to bond with the males my age meant that I dropped out of sport altogether. I'd make excuses for not doing PE, decline offers of a kickabout or any sort of competitive activity; even *Mortal Kombat* was too much pressure for me.

Puberty hit and my once super-speedy child metabolism phase was over. The Findus Crispy Pancakes, KitKats and Viennettas I used to obliterate into thin air had found me. And they were hanging off my chin. I was built differently to the rest of my family – unclear why. Our Jane and Andrew, not content with being textbook students, were also textbook sizes, all long and lean with unquenchable appetites. Our Jane prefers two breakfasts to the daily recommended serving of one; she'd scoff down potato cakes laden with butter, crumpets near-translucent with melting Lurpak on, before having a slice of cake with a brew, while managing to maintain the figure of a ballerina. I, on the other hand, hit twelve and adopted the body of my father. Not the athletic one he'd had as a youth but the one he had now. The one of a nearing-sixty-year-old bread-loving OAP. I had a fat round head, no shoulders and a pot belly. The rest of the family were like models from a CK One advert; why was I curving round into myself like a shy armadillo? While the other boys at school were growing into their bodies nicely, I was going full Pugsley. Everyone managed to have skinheads and look like the Hot Felon, whereas my skinhead was giving shaved jacket potato. Barry From *EastEnders*. I was beginning to be aware of my body and my family started to notice too.

Imagine at the peak of your teenage insecurity, shying away from the bullies at school, shielding your gayness, and concealing your body, to come home to 'All right, Fat Boy Roy? How was school?'

FAT! BOY! ROY! Can you imagine?!

It is a testament to my love for my family and our extreme closeness that I've never thought it was offensive or felt like it was mean – until . . . well, now. My dad and Our Jane would call me for dinner with an orchestral swing of 'Fat Boy Roy', said with smiling faces, and off I'd go, skipping down for another delicious frozen crispy pancake delight, totally missing the severity of the body-shaming moniker they had bestowed on me. In hindsight it could've been absolutely devastating to a teenager going through puberty, finding their feet and trying to fit into their body, but it seemed to me to be water off a duck's back. Maybe in comparison to the fear of showing any kind of gayness in daily life at school it seemed warm: 'Ahhh cute, a nickname!' Maybe. Plus I think it stood me in good stead for all the mud-slinging, name-calling and utter shite that you receive when you willingly put yourself in the public eye.

During my time at home living under the alias of Fat Boy Roy, not content with the giant head, baby-like physique and flat forehead, my body decided to add one more out-of-sync string to its already unbalanced bow. My teeth. Rather than drop out like a regular child's, my milk teeth hung on in there until secondary school like an unwanted politician in office. Hell-bent on staying put, refusing to evacuate and fucking up the entire plan, aka my face being remotely attractive. My grown-up teeth had no other option: they had to stage an attack. Starting to force themselves through my gums. Starting to appear ABOVE my stupid, idle baby teeth, the whiteness of the new guys starting to glimmer behind my pink fleshy gums and looking giant in comparison to the old guys. I finally got the movie star looks I was after; I now looked like I could star in *Pan's Labyrinth*.

The look was a unique one, a dual layer of teeth, both fighting for attention. Jaggedy baby ones underneath and giant grown up ones above all cramped up over one another. A PERFECT look for when you're at the most self-conscious age of your life. There was a lot going on in there, a gruesome orgy of teeth all fighting for attention. I was gutted and did everything I could to hide what was happening. I'd talk into my hand and tilt my head to the floor when speaking. Or try to hold my mouth and speak, like a great thinker would. I was so embarrassed about it I tried to keep it secret from everyone and it's probably the longest I've ever kept my mouth shut. My family were made aware when I had my school photos done and it was apparent when they saw the results that something was wrong. They looked at my photo with bemusement. It was weird because it kind of didn't look like me. You know when one of the *Real Housewives* has had *something* done to their face but you just can't place it? It was like that. They questioned what it was, why I was making such an odd expression, pursed lips and a fake smile that resulted in a kind of sassy/secretive look. I pulled my lips up and showed them my new fangs to a wave of great noise: a mixture of hilarity and disgust.

'WOLF BOY HOHOWWOWOWOWHOOOOOOW-LLLLLL,' Our Jane screamed, bursting out laughing, before my dad joined in with a 'HOOOOOOOWWWLLLLLL,' head tipping up to the sky.

After a trip to the dentist for a slip-in/slip-out brace that I eventually lost in McDonald's, the teeth found their place and Wolf Boy was dropped, with Fat Boy Roy or more commonly just 'Roy' becoming my go-to name. Over the next few years I made little or no attempt to shed the name or the weight. Even in sixth form when lads started to socialise by spending time at the gym, my body shape was something I felt I'd inherited and there was nothing I could do about it. It's genetic, I thought! Yeh it's genetic that I like eating Club biscuits. It wasn't until university that I became truly conscious of my shape. I'd never compared myself to other boys at school because it was too extreme – I didn't see myself akin to them, we didn't get each other, I didn't get their passion for United or girls and they didn't get my passion for Gloria Estefan. So I felt we were almost different species.

Uni truly was the first time where I thought 'oh my God look at my body' for the first time. Thrown into the deep end of adult life days ahead of my 18th birthday, I met people from all walks of life, who would cook stir-fries or go for a jog. It was only then that I thought about maybe eating some vegetables and maybe having a glass of water. Seriously. I do genuinely not remember having one glass of water in the 1990s. I'd entered a new magical world of hydration. After I started my dad would scream, 'You're mad on the stuff!' every time I came home, excited by the thrill of fresh, soft, Mancunian tap water.

My childhood was spent obsessing over pop stars' aesthetics but I never once thought about how I looked until university . . . I realised I looked terrible. My first year look was totally wild. My hair was long at the sides and back with a swipe-across shorter fringe. I didn't have a reference, I just knew I wanted it long as a demonstration of my dedication to the Libertines. I thought it was giving Carl Barât when in fact it was more your Auntie Carol. This wig-like mop I was rocking was paired with rimless glasses, the kind a middle-aged architect might wear on *Grand Designs*, and my head was larger than ever, marinated and swollen with lager.

One day in the student union for our regular lunch of multiple pints, a cheesy panini and a flapjack or two, my friend Grainne said, 'You know pints make you fat?'

'What? Alcohol? Makes you fat? Doubt it.' Surely not, look at Sid and Nancy I thought, right skinny them two.

She said it was true and that she was concerned that we were entering our Wayne and Waynetta Slob era. Grainne suggested we go on a diet. But we only eat flapjacks, how can we be fat? I thought. My ignorance was truly bliss. I argued that flapjacks were diet food cos they have oats in them – they're good for you? Surely!

We were not being healthy, so we decided to make big changes. We were going to be new people and be living to the best of our potential. We did what anyone did back then for life and diet advice: we turned to *Heat* magazine. A near bible of the time, it told us that anyone who was anyone was on the Atkins Diet. We didn't know what it was but we were sold! 'What is it? What's the science?' We didn't know and we didn't care, we just thought it was incredibly glamorous for two ravers in their late teens to take it on.

Now before the now legendary *TOWIE* quote 'no carbs before Marbs' made it a mainstream thing, the idea of not having carbs was mad. I mean what else was there to eat? Cutting out bread, potatoes, pints and pies from your diet seemed CRAZY. Like CRAZY. Especially to northerners. We felt like scientists. From Japan. In the future. It made me feel incredibly modern taking on this new regime. It gave me a sense of independence and power never harboured before. I felt like a fat Steve Jobs. I was high knowing that I was onto something, harnessing a superpower over the bread-eating idiots who surrounded us.

Later that week I went on a family holiday to Lanzarote with all the Grimmys, my first time back with them since I'd started uni. I wanted this holiday to change me. I wanted to go back to uni as a different person. I wanted it to be my Sandy-in-leather moment from *Grease*. I'd step off the train at Liverpool Lime Street and everyone would be open-mouthed as they crashed their convertibles in awe, while the jocks howled to the sky like wolves, stomping their feet and pulling their leather jacket sleeves up to their elbows. Or something like that.

It was a buffet dinner situation at the hotel and I helped myself to chicken, fish and vegetables and explained to my parents the 'science' behind it. 'Science? You're hungry, that's why you lose weight,' Dad argued. I mean, great point. I stuck to it and SHOCK HORROR a fortnight off the pints, pizzas, flapjacks and fags does wonders for you. For the first time in my life I felt confident in how I looked. I remember going back to Liverpool and seeing a Rimmel advert on a bus whizz past me: 'Get the London look!' it said. Already got it thanks darrrrliiiiinnn!

Strutting around without my double chin gave me a new lease of life. Gone were the oversized baggy cargo trousers and in came women's spray-on jeans from Topshop, I shed the trackie tops for vests and see-through shirts and started dabbling in trilby hats now my face could fit under them. For the first time ever I didn't just not-mind looking at pictures of myself, I actually liked it. Ahhhh, vanity!

Like a chunky caterpillar I'd broken out of my carbohydrate chrysalis and now felt the power of giant butterfly-like wings upon my back. Ready to take flight.

Losing weight and, more importantly, losing my charming family nickname gave me a sense of control. It was my first foray into self-care and self-control, something I'd neglected for my previous twenty years. My clothes, diet, size, nicknames, how I held myself were all dictated by someone else, and now I was in this state of flux where anything seemed possible. I realised I'd spent most of my teenage years wishing to be someone else, daydreaming the days away. I'd wasted time bleeding into other people's business or priorities or dipping into different person-alities, but I felt different now, empowered, tuned in to myself and ready for a new stage of my life. It felt like I was ready to be me. My dreams of radio, while still a dream, felt more focused and real. If I could defy the gravitational pull of the dessert cart at an all-inclusive in Lanzarote I could do anything.

5

Little Gay Me

I never thought I'd be happy gay.

Now I worry I'm not gay enough and wish I was gayer, that I could level up to another dimension of faggotry.

But back when I was ten in the mid-nineties, when I was figuring myself out, I wasn't overjoyed at the prospect of being 'a gay'. Growing up I just learnt from somewhere that being gay was something to be really sad about, something dark and full of holy sin. It seemed like a terrible affliction.

Now I'm a fully functional adult gay I'm content in my queerness, but Little Gay Me couldn't see through the death sentence AIDS ads and the shame. I didn't look up to any deeply iconic gays or see the queer community in its full multifaceted fabulousness. I just felt the weight of resentment towards the queers from the world around me and felt the pressure of this internalised secret building up on my closeted shoulders.

I was taught the Catholic way of life, reciting prayers and promising to give our lives over to our Lord and Saviour Jesus Christ. I went to two Roman Catholic Church schools, the first named after not one but two saints – Saint Aidan & Oswald's RC Primary – before moving on to the quite camply named

Our Lady's RC High. If the name 'Our Lady's Roman Catholic High' is conjuring up images of the Sarah Michelle Gellar classic *Cruel Intentions*, then stop. Because before you start imagining stone staircases with stained-glass windows, it was a post-war ugly 60s concrete monstrosity of a building with all the charm of a cardboard box.

Rather than scented Catholic incense there was an overwhelming STENCH of decaying sewage that really kicked off in the corridor to the canteen. It was a smell I have never smelt anywhere else since. Not even at Glastonbury.

It was the school that asbestos built.

As you can tell, I didn't exactly LOVE it. I thought school was boring and uninspiring. I couldn't wait to leave. It's hard to sit and remember solid memories of my school years because I was never really mentally present there. I was off-me-'ead daydreaming of being free. The irony being that twenty-five years on now I *am* 'free', all I want to do is learn stuff. I have an insatiable thirst for knowledge – if only there was an institution that catered for this in my life . . .?

I liked primary school, gleefully running around with the girls, but big school felt aggressive. It felt competitive and it was exhausting. Not the learning. It was exhausting because you were always looking over your shoulder for a beating, waiting for someone to trick you or trip you up. Exhausting because I was taking on this everlasting performance of trying to fit in, of trying to be what I thought a teenage lad should be. Exhausting because I spent my time at secondary school mainly trying to keep the lid on the fact that I was slowly realising I was a massive gay.

And every now and then the lid would blow off as I'd do a high-kick impersonating Margarita Pracatan or pick the wrong crowd and ask them if they'd seen Mariah Carey on *Top of The Pops* and if they hadn't I'd do a little impression for them. And while I loved lad-approved Oasis, Tupac and Biggie, I couldn't deny that 'I'M EVERY WOMAN IT'S ALL IN MEEEEE' was an absolute banger and raised this one day in maths class, to a rapturous onslaught of pointing and laughing at my expense. Why I thought straight teenage lads at my comprehensive in Oldham would like me singing it to them still plagues my mind. To be fair, it was worth taking an emotional beating for, it still standing as one of my all-time favourite songs.

The gayness was starting to ooze out of me and back then anything that wasn't rock-hard masculinity was 'gay' and that was a bad thing. If you weren't chowing down on a Yorkie bar and beating someone up while wanking over Rachel Stevens you were 'GAY!'

Any sort of femininity was scowled at with a cutting 'soft lad!' As if being a 'hard lad' was the only proper, approved, viable way to live. Over the years the 'soft lad' taunts amounted to me realising that my girly ways and need to do a Tina Turner drag show from time to time were somehow making me soft. And that wasn't good. It wasn't normal. So I was led to believe that I was in some way odd. And wrong. Two great feelings to fester in my juvenile mind.

I don't know if being called a soft lad was meant to change my mind and give me a heterosexualising kick up the arse. To instil some sort of need for textbook masculinity in me; but it actually did the opposite. I found solace in my softness. I hated the thought of being hard. It was actually more realistic for my brain to pretend to be Tina Turner than it was to be a hard lad at school.

So for a while I thought I should have been a girl. I was told I had 'girly legs', played football 'like a girl' and spoke like a girl. I didn't understand why they thought I was such a 'girl'. I thought maybe there'd been a mistake and I'd been born into the wrong body. I mean maybe Eileen did a magic trick and gave me a girl's brain and a man's willy? Maybe I was both? During bath time I'd check to see if I didn't actually have a vagina, as I couldn't understand why seemingly everyone couldn't accept me as a boy.

Once out of the bath there was nothing I found more exciting than making a glamorous up-do from a towel curled up on my head. I'd pull up my face to give me cat eyes and clip on Eileen's giant gold earrings from the 80s and lip-sync to Gloria Estefan in the mirror.

I started to notice I was not following the standard gender norms for a boy my age. My friends were not up for making a ladies' haircut out of a towel and doing a show. The things I loved, they hated. They thought *The Little Mermaid* was shit. Deeply offended, I wanted to watch it over and over. I imitated Ariel on the rocks by wrapping my legs together in swimming lessons in an attempt to become my ginger female icon.

I'd beg to watch it at sleepovers at friends' houses, passionately pitching the merits of the film before the ultimate conversation-ender from my friends:

'THAT'S
FOR
GIRLS
NOT
BOYS'

I'd suffer in silence and have to watch wrestling. When it was time to play *Street Fighter* I just had to be Chun-Li. It was time for me to live outside my tubby pre-teen self and become this digitally created lady. I don't know how but I was relating more to this fictional character than to actual human boys. I loved being Chun-Li, the white knee-high boots with a kitten heel, the crotch-skimming dress and the white ribbons in her hair, flowing delicately in the digitally created wind. I'd stand on my tiptoes pretending to be her in mock fights – 'Hhhhhhii-ya!' imagining the knee-high boots delivering an almighty blow to my imaginary hard male opponent.

In hindsight, the signs were there. I'm laughing now at how gay Little Gay Me really was then. The list of things I loved ran like a dream night at the Mighty Hoopla: Tina Turner, Gloria Estefan and Kylie. But at that time I didn't equate these loves with being gay. I didn't realise that while forming these bonds to these female gay icons, I was shying away from the laddiness of boys at school.

All these women I idolised on telly were glamourous and expressive, open and engaging, and my image of men was emotionless footballers talking on *Match of The Day*, holding in any signs of passion or personality. Men felt hard and women felt soft. I certainly didn't feel hard.

Although I was leaning into my softness, I wouldn't say I identified as being gay yet. I didn't see the correlation between me loving all these iconically camp things and having sexual intercourse with a man. Being gay seemed like a foreign, physical act, not a way of life, so when people called me gay at school I was genuinely confused.

'Me? Gay? Erm, I have a Geri Halliwell bookmark! If I was gay would I have a Geri Halliwell bookmark??!' (Well yes dear, you would). I'd clip-clop off in my gold-buckled Russell & Bromley school shoes, shaking my bowl cut fringe out of my eyes. I guess the other kids knew before I knew.

Twelve-year-old me would get the bus home and think about what the kids had said. Gay? Me? But I love girls: all the girls at school, Kylie, Ginger Spice AND Tina Turner. Surely I couldn't be gay, I thought? That would be mad! No one is gay in Oldham. Gays live in New York in the 80s.

It just seemed so mad to be a gay! So out of this world. Being gay was painted as some other worldy life which ran alongside 'normal' life, in a different lane, never to be crossed. This 'normal life' was presented to me on the daily. I saw it on the telly, on Corrie and through my front window as I stared out at the other families. Normal life was nice enough. You had a job and a wife and two kids. At the weekend you'd go to the football with your mate, Steve, he too living his very own perfect normal life. Then off to the pub where you'd sit with your legs wide open and have a pint. I couldn't really imagine me with this life, I didn't have a Steve and I didn't want to sit with my legs open. I wanted to constantly cross them over one another until somebody mentioned how thin my ankles were. (Still do this.)

Then there was this gay life. This was the antithesis to normal life. Gays were sentenced to a life of raving on drugs in Canal Street with no families, dancing away their sadness in T-shirts that were too small for them. It was something I didn't want. I loved my family and all my family friends; were they going to disown me and send me off for a sordid life of gay misery? I was racked with worry.

Now our family weren't a conservative family – we swore, we drank, we screamed at each other, we played music loud, we liked crude comedy, so we were not the Waltons. And while Manchester's Canal Street was a mere few miles away, we lived in suburban Oldham, so I had minimal interaction with anyone gay. My footy-loving dad and brother both showed love for the gays growing up; Pete loved Elton John, George Michael and Boy George. 'A fantastic artist is that Boy George.' And Our Andrew praised the clubbing skills of the gays, saying they knew how to party properly, and he and his girlfriend would take to the dancefloor of Paradise Club till dawn. So the key lads in my life offered *some* comfort. Their approval of gay culture took the hard edge off a bit. But the gays were still othered, still the not-normals, the outsiders.

And as celebrated as they were, I always felt that there was a tinge of sadness towards them by the rest of the world. 'Poor buggers.'

There were some real-life gays near us, Bob and Freddy, and my dad bonded with them over a shared love of the classic old-man pursuits, whether gay or straight: gardening and golf. They were referred to by everyone as 'Gay Bob' or 'Gay Freddy.' Like Postman Pat, their thing became them. I'd cycle past and tell new visitors, 'The gays live there,' like we were passing royalty. Then I'd say, 'They're nice though.'

THEY'RE

NICE

THOUGH

!!!

The homophobic smog in the air had already infiltrated my own pre-teen body.

The thought of future me being defined by my sexuality as Gay Nick gave me the ick. I didn't appreciate Bob and Freddy at the time but in hindsight they were deeply chic. They had an immaculately curated garden of lush roses, with perfectly pruned hedges, and wore freshly pressed shirts tucked into their chinos. They were a John Waters dream. I wish I'd spoken to them more and taken in their happy life in action; it could've nursed a lot of pain. I remember thinking it was all right for them to be gay – they were old and didn't have to go to school.

I did and I started to feel sick to my core as the realisation that I might not fancy girls began to descend over me.

It didn't happen instantly, it kind of happened in reverse. I didn't wake up one day and feel like I was ready to jump on a Pride float and go gay clubbing, it was a slow, painful realisation that started when I didn't really get Page 3. And every other boy at school very much did. I'd hear the noises of 'phwoarr' from lads when they caught a glimpse of Kimberly, nineteen from Kent's, jugs, and try as I might to conjure up some sort of response I'd just think, hmmm Kimberly I don't really like yer knickers. No offence Kimberly, it was a classic case of it's not you, it's me. There were a few things at school where my heterosexuality was tested: sport, public speaking, school dances, and the pinnacle being the annual 100 Sexiest Women In The World in *FHM*.

It was a run-down of 100 perfectly presented girls in tiny lingerie, maybe bent over a neon Lamborghini or attempting to seductively do the washing up with foam on their nips.

The day the issue dropped was like a big straight Christmas of hetero horninesss. It caused Beatlemania-style crushes down at the newsagents and was presented in a black paper wallet like ancient Sanskrit. While the lads were frothing at the mouth over Gail Porter and Kelly Brook, I'd go through and pick which knickers and bra set I'd wear if I were a girl. Oooh, that neon one is fun, I'd think to myself.

I worried I didn't fancy them like the other boys did. I wrote it off as these women were simply too hot for my simple tastes. I decided my brain couldn't possibly fancy them as they were these extreme visions of the feminine form that a simple Oldham lad couldn't fathom.

I still didn't think I was gay then, I thought I just hadn't found the right woman. But I did start to notice that it was proving near impossible to find one who got me going. Come December, every female celebrity would inexplicably take all their clothes off for a photoshoot next to an impossibly small set of dates and call it a calendar. I don't know why aged twelve you'd need a calendar, but everyone was mad for them back then.

'Which calendar are you gonna get?' Such a hard choice of which naked lady should adorn my wall for the next year when I really didn't want them up there in the first place. I had absolutely jack shit to write in a calendar apart from 'school' and 'home'.

Each year mums would ask their sons which pin-up they'd like this year, buying soft porn disguised as an admin tool. They'd go for Melinda Messenger or Jet From *Gladiators*. I got on board in an effort to disguise my gayness and thought I'd ask for a woman that straights would like: Kylie.

Now Kylie of course is sexy and hot and fancied by the straights, but she is also the gayest woman in the world. It did little to hide the gay, I might as well have asked for a Liza Minnelli calendar. (Note to self: order Liza Minnelli calendar.)

Back then, on Saturday mornings I'd join Eileen on her errands: Martins for ham butties and strawberry tarts, then we'd swing by the butchers, the fishmongers and Somerfield for bits before the newsagents to pay for the paper man and a pick 'n' mix. I was always drawn to the aisle of magazines, colours and shapes flooding my eyes; I loved anything striking and graphic and wanted to take them all home with me. This little corner shop was a wondrous place of inspiration for Little Gay Me – there I'd see iconic graphic images on the covers of *The Face*, *ID* and *Vogue*. It was a window into another world, another world of seeing other life out there in vivid technicolour.

Every now and then I'd substitute my sweets for a magazine and I'd get to pick what I brought home, not understanding *The Face* but being drawn to its vibrancy. This one morning I inexplicably chose a football magazine. Though I wasn't into football, everyone else was, so, not wanting to be the odd one out, I was still hoping that one day I might fall in love with this beautiful (boring) game.

I got my magazine and headed back to the car, flicking through the pages and pages of football terms I didn't understand. I read about tricks I could try at home to make me a better player, thinking I could master these in the back garden and wow everyone at school the next time I was forced to partake. I read it with the same enthusiasm as you do homework. It wasn't natural and it didn't make sense. As I flicked through, I became more and more over it – until something caught my eye.

It stopped me in my tracks and made me feel funny in my stomach. It was sharp and precise. A feeling I hadn't felt before. One of sickness and panic. I was struck with disbelief; it was both refreshing and unnerving, like a physical convulsion vibrating all of my cells. But I couldn't look away, I couldn't understand it, dumbstruck in disbelief.

Similar to that fish in *Finding Nemo*, I was blinded, I was hypnotised to a place of no return. After pages of boring pictures of referees and balls, this was the therapeutic healing my eyeballs needed. I had never seen anything like this in my life. And I could not look away, totally magnetised to this near-religious experience I was witnessing with my own eyes.

It was a black and white close-up picture of David Beckham post-match in a bath, swiping back his hair with his hands and looking directly at me and deep into my now very homosexual soul.

We pulled up at home. I was now feeling physically sick from the mixture of looking down for the entire car ride and seeing David's face for the first time.

I walked into the house and sat down, magazine still in hand and eyeballs still full of the good stuff. Still unable to look away. I was starting to go cross-eyed à la magic eye pictures and I stared at it so intently and for so long that a magic phrase started to appear:

'YOU'RE A MASSIVE GAY,' it said.

Time passed, the sun set and rose again and here I was still transfixed on this image. Taking my eyes from his face for the first time in what felt like millennia, I popped into Eileen's room, where she was doing her make-up in the mirror.

'Mum, would you look at this?' I asked. 'Isn't it a beautiful photograph?' my prepubescent naivety still believing that I was genuinely excited by the composition of the image and not the bloody drop-dead-gorgeous cheekbones of Goldenballs.

'. . . that? Oh . . . yes, it's a nice photograph,' she replied, baffled and slightly startled.

'I love it. I can't stop looking at it,' I said, 'can I put it on my wall?'

She looked hesitant, not angry or disapproving; but a look of concern glazed her face. I felt like I shouldn't be looking at it for some reason, or that I'd looked at it for too long.

It was at this point that my mum had to think about what this meant. Her twelve-year-old son who has never had any interest in football now wants to pin up a footballer on the wall. However, this is not a photo of Pelé scoring at the World Cup or George Best lifting a trophy, it's soon-to-be gay icon David Beckham naked in a foamy bath with smouldering come-to-bed eyes in what looks like a Steven Klein shoot.

Her response was iconic in hindsight: 'Go ask your dad.'

Maybe she thought this was something for him to hear from me, something he could witness direct from the horse's mouth, a clear graphic of spotting my gayness in childhood, a moment he could relish, realising who I was as a person. Or maybe she just wanted to do her make-up in peace.

I went to find him in the garden. He was up a ladder with an electric tree clipper trimming a conifer. Classic dad business.

'Dad, can I put this up on my wall?' opening up the double-page spread of doe-eyed David peering from his foamy bath.

'Yeh but don't use bloody Sellotape on yer bleedin' wallpaper or it'll all come off.'

Did he see it? Did he approve? Did he even take it in?

I didn't overthink it. I went inside and carefully but forcefully plucked the centre pages from the magazine, laying David's face flat down on the table and carefully rolling up four tiny balls of Blu Tack for each corner. I stuck him directly above my bed. Before carefully removing him to a better location at the side of my bed so I could lie and look at him.

It was a funny feeling of realisation. In the fantasy side of my brain I was overjoyed that David Beckham existed in the world and that I could fall in love with him in the safety of my own bedroom. The reality side of my brain, which I tried to close off, was in turmoil. I didn't love the framing of the photo or the way it was shot, I loved it because David Beckham was the perfect prime example of a man. And I fancied him. I fancied men.

The fantasy of the allure of Beckham was serotonin-inducing, an intoxicating, overwhelming teenage crush that made me red in the face, but the reality of realising I was gay was crushing.

Ugh, I was gutted.

Being gay was a disappointing result to little me: why meeee, oh for God's sake, of course I would be gay. Can't having asthma, needing glasses and having freckles be enough? Now I have the burden of being a gay to contend with as well? GREAT.

My stomach was in knots, churning over and over like before you sit an exam you know you've not revised for.

I was too young to analyse the feelings I was having, so they were reduced by me internally to being just wrong. My feelings were wrong, my life was wrong and now everything was going to go wrong. It was a lot to take on. A heady mix of guilt and shame meant I felt I was carrying this dark weight around with me as I navigated my way around school, nervously trying to hold in this brewing sickness I'd created in my head. My throat would close up, shoulders tighten and my jaw lock, something I still do now; I have to forcibly relax my head and breathe out. I was dreading my class finding out, my family finding out, anyone finding out, and conjured up devastating visions of the sad gay journey ahead. Alone living in gay holy sin. (Camp!)

I thought I'd done something wrong to deserve this, praying to my crucifix (which was on the wall inches above David's face), asking why God would put such a curse on me. I prayed each night to be made normal, to be made straight. I'd kneel at the side of my bed in your classic prayer stance, my knees jutting into the wooden floors of my bedroom, and pray to the Lord, Our Father that he would rid me of this plight. Tears would form in my eyes as I begged the highest being to fix his mistake. I went to sleep all hot and bothered hoping tomorrow it would be different.

PLOT SPOILER: it didn't work. It's almost as if God's not real. Or maybe he was out that night when I needed him most, crying on the floor of my childhood bedroom begging for him to right his wrong. After all, he created me, remember, this was his fault, so why choose to ignore me? I took it that my sin was so vile that even God himself couldn't help. He could create a world in six days and handcraft billions of humans, but I was soooooo gay, there was nothing he could do about it. What a rinse. It was the only thing I prayed for. And it didn't work. So I decided to knock the praying on the head.

At school and weekly trips to church it raged on, though. I hated going to church, the smell of it, the sound of it, the rules of it, the muted depressing hum of an organ that probably need-ed tuning.

We learnt about crucifixion, about living to serve God, and sang songs about leaving your friends and family to follow the ways of Jesus Christ. We were told that if you were good in this life, you got a good afterlife in heaven. (The cloud, not the gay nightclub). But I was gay. So was I about to embark on a bad life? How could I be good if I was gay? And if I was bad, there was only one place I could end up: hell.

So I began to think that this life was going to be full of shame, guilt and sin and my afterlife would be me down in hell on my own, while my family would be all together in heaven living a life free from sin.

Fucking nightmare.

At school we were given a handy guide on what to do and what not to do, called the Ten Commandments; we were at the mercy of God, his way or the highway. My ignored prayers felt as though he had chosen to send me down the highway alone.

Growing up in Catholic churches and schools I never thought that God Hated Fags more than the next man, just that everyone hated them the same. Then late one night I saw a holy vision that made me believe. A woman running across a hillside fell to the ground as crucifixes lit up in flames. It was Madonna. Not Madonna the Mother Of Jesus, the other Madonna, from New York's Danceteria. The one thing I'll thank the Catholic Church for is the references it allowed Madonna to steal. In the depths of my now teenage self-disdain, I saw her frolicking with gays on her bed in the movie *In Bed With Madonna*. She hugged them, she kissed them on the mouth, she loved them. So I loved her. The sweet highness of her voice was an elixir for the weight of the world around

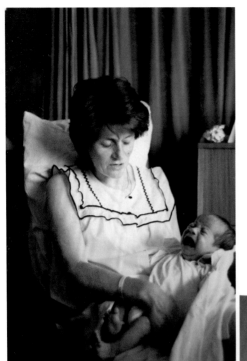

Eileen welcomed a very loud, annoying arrival in the summer of 1984 (me).

Can't believe I met David Bowie.

I peaked here; the best I've ever looked.

Prime soft lad.
I need to bring
this haircut back.

My first day at school
and I was a little shit.

My First Day at School

my mum took me to school
on my first DAY! my
first friend was Katie
I was excited to play
in the sand pits and
the Toys. My second
frend was Neil. My
teacher tresch was Mrs Bebb.
I bitbit my finger and
said some-one else did it.
when I came home my
gran picd me up from
school. We got the Bus
from school. We had
chips for tea and then
my mum come home.
I watched the kids
tvi and went to bed.

Absolutely wasted
after losing my
trousers somewhere in
Greece in 1993. Sad.

No teeth, just vibes.

The perfect holiday destination for any toddler: the Berlin Wall. Seen here with my childhood heroes: Our Andrew and Our Jane.

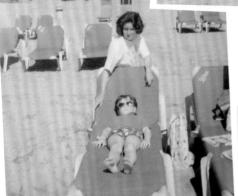

Glad we got up early to reserve these beds. It looks packed.

Eileen made it to 41 before having me, then had to deal with this energy every day after work. Apologies.

Feeling loved with Mum and Dad on one of our mini-breaks for three.

Hang this in the Louvre (sorry Eileen).

Was randomly obsessed with camels as a child. Even more randomly, here we are riding them in Lanzarote.

Why do we look like we're from a Netflix documentary about a family that murders a small mining town in Middle America?

Off to a family wedding on the street I grew up on, looking like a funeral director.

Look how happy I was to be in a Man United kit. Go sports!

With the siblings Grim at another family party. I seemed to constantly be at parties and was always thrilled to be there.

My first true love: Sandy, the living, breathing dustbin dog.

Mum, Dad and Gran surprised me with a visit at uni. I had a surprise for them too: I hadn't been to bed for two days and looked like this.

A big moment for me was my first lads' holiday to Ibiza aged 16, and my first famous DJ encounter: Brandon Block.

Mairead, Tabitha and Jenny: the ladies who taught me how to party (with mixed results).

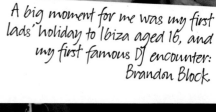

In my student radio days, meeting radio demi-god Zane Lowe.

My first ever meeting with Annie Mac at Glastonbury 2004. I haven't left her alone since.

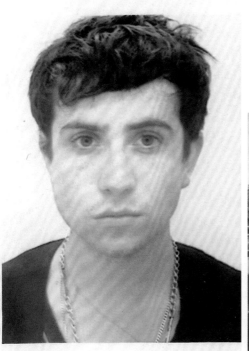

Baby indie sleaze me.

Listens to The Libertines once...

The Hawley Arms in 2006,
where Ray-Bans, waistcoats
and black-and-white film
were enforced by indie law.

Professional TV hosts
preparing for a day of
filming by spending the
night before like this.

Charlie's Angels:
Camden Edition.

Baby Adele and me,
quite literally 'When
We Were Young'.

Another relaxing
night out with
wallflowers Jaime
Winstone and
Lily Allen.

me; it made me feel lighter and cleaner. I decided to convert to the church of Madonna Ciccone. Finally, a religious icon I could relate to; she was loud, she was obtuse, she was a Leo baby born in mid-August – just like me. I swapped my nightly prayers for nightly affirmations as I danced around my room to 'Express Yourself' and 'Human Nature', finding every word of these pop prayers life-affirming to Little Gay Me.

6

Bigger Gay Me

I'd like to say that I heard Madonna once and my internalised gay shame dissolved into thin air, but alas, try as I might to Express Myself, I bloody couldn't.

Whereas Little Gay Me wanted to rid myself of my queerness, now I find myself worrying that I'm not gay enough and that I look like a Foxtons agent when I go to Dalston for a gay night out. When I was a kid I was worried any slight movement gave off a HYPER-GAY ENERGY like a carbon copy of Elton in Ru Paul drag, whereas nowadays I feel like Mr Bean in gay clubs.

I'm annoyed at myself that I wasted so many years wishing I wasn't gay and squashing down the fabulousness of it all. Being gay is fabulous. Genuinely. Hindsight is, as we know, a wonderful thing because being gay actually spurred me on to great things. It made me want to make my dreams come true as a fuck-you to everyone. It made me want to push myself into uncomfortable situations because I was already uncomfortable. I was already embarrassed. I couldn't get any lower. I was happy to plod on to accomplish my dreams with (pun intended) gay abandon cos guess what, after you've been made to feel like shit for all of the days in your teenage life so far, what's one more?

Feeling like the odd one out went one of two ways. I'd either fold in on myself, believing that yes I was a freak and deserved to die, or go totally the other way, believing in myself more than I believed in anything else. My self-belief was so strong that I had NO doubt in my mind that I could do whatever I wanted to do with my life. I KNEW I wouldn't stay on the outskirts of the city, I knew I couldn't last long in suburbia.

It wasn't always this easy. My brain was, and still is, at war with itself. My internal monologue is on a relentless merry-go-round, flitting between being my biggest fan and my biggest troll. I guess it's manageable now as an adult, but it wasn't so great when I was young, figuring out my queerness.

Once I fought my way out of my teens I still struggled with accepting my sexual destiny. Gay love felt impossible. AS IF. I'd joke about marrying a man with my female friends and the thought of Eileen with a hat on as I walked up the aisle to 'Here Comes The Bride' used to set us off pissing ourselves. Well now I'm getting married. To a man. And although Eileen will wear a hat, I probably won't walk up the aisle to church bells. This is growth; I no longer hysterically laugh at my own potential happiness. Back then, laughing at the wild notion of me finding love with a man was deflecting. I wasn't wearing my gay cape with pride. I was sort of wearing it underneath 'straight clothes' and letting a flash out every now and then.

Even though I was out to my friends and having a lol at gay clubs, I was still resenting it. Not on a surface level, but deep down. Where it counts. You see, you spend long enough listening to shit about gays and, even as one, you start to believe it.

Once I got to the going-out-out age of nineteen I spiralled. My gayness made me want to be destructive, it made me mad, it made me want to be a mess, it made me want to self-sabotage so that this could be the thing that was heavy, not the gayness.

I tried to love myself more but the contempt was a cloud I couldn't shake off; I wanted rid of it but also, as it was the only weather I knew, I clung onto it for dear life. I started to enjoy the resentment I felt towards myself, happily going out but using it as a vehicle for getting fucked up. I sat in my feelings of worthlessness to the point that I was overwhelmed and so angry at being gay.

Basically, yer girl was a mess. I had sort of surrounded myself with other messes too. We were a little gaggle of wasters all self-medicating with booze and blackouts and claiming 'it was lol'. Was it though? Doesn't sound toooo funny in hindsight. Why was I doing this? I felt loved. I felt surrounded by friends. My family called me every day. It wasn't their problem, their doing, this was all on me. I just didn't like myself and it had to stop. I'd have waves of good days and then WHACK a wave of bad days and I'd go under, lost at sea for a while. Then I saw a lighthouse. It had a flashing logo on it. It was an E4 logo. Lol but true.

Work was my saviour really. I started getting a bit of TV work on E4 – daunting, but also reassuring in that someone had seen something in me. It meant I now had an opportunity to actually make my radio dreams come true; the path had become murky and blurred but this little bit of telly felt like it put me back on track. If I wanted to do it I had to fix up. A bit.

I started caring about how I looked, about being a better friend, about showering, about checking in on my family, all these things I'd neglected in my pity party. I was booked and busy and rather than wasting my time thinking about how I felt I was just concerned with how Estelle and Kate Nash were doing and when their albums were out. You know, serious stuff like that. I joke but it actually was great for me – it pushed me out of my comfort zone constantly; meeting famous people and having to disarm them on television made me think nothing was as scary as THAT.

The job validated me. The pressure was on to perform but the more I was myself, the better the reaction I got from my production team and guests. Then the bosses were happier, and the channel too. It meant I got more work. I was slowly realising that it wasn't just OK to be myself, it was actually essential, to me and to the career that I so badly longed for. I'd spent years doing the exact opposite but now I had seen the light. It was a life-saver. It dragged me from the depths. Funny the first things I loved – telly and radio – were the things to help free me from my own mental turmoil.

Work was going well, I was finally comfortable in my own gay skin. The hurdle was to accept that I could be loved by and be in love with a man. I was worried that deep down I was a massive homophobic, god-fearing Republican. I was avoiding the fact that REALLY I was unwilling to date, to fall in love, to learn, to be with a gay man. Instead, I pinned my hopes on men I could never be with: James Dean, who's dead, or Leonardo DiCaprio, who is alive but might as well be dead to me due to his passionate love of vagina.

I was creating more barriers to reaching gay nirvana and, more annoyingly, wasting good gay time crying over The James Deans and The Leo DiCaps telling myself IT WAS SO UNFAIR THAT THESE MEN I LOVED DID NOT LOVE ME BACK. The drama! I crossed over into my twenties and celebrated by moping, living out my days like a tortured, heartbroken Shakespearean character. Probably Bottom. A wise older gay told me to not waste my time and that fancying straight men and hooking your hopes and dreams on them was a road well-trodden by himself, and it's a long and lonely one and I should probably get off it. Easier said than done. He suggested that I was deflecting emotions of some sort, that I was fearing blooming into the big healthy, happy homo that I deserved to be by being lost in the impossible possibility of these relationships to whine and pine over. I tried to explain this to a female straight friend of mine recently.

'Is it like falling in love with a married man?' she asked.

'No, cos a married man might leave his wife for you.' I said. 'It's more like falling in love with a door. Or a rock.'

I was pinning my hopes on something I knew deep down could never happen, my inner saboteur subconsciously delaying my progress as a fully functional adult who want-ed love and (more importantly) self-love. They say you can never love someone else unless you love yourself. Well, I must have bloody hated myself because I wasted some of the best years of my life crying over stupid (but quite fit) straight people. A delaying tactic in the self-acceptance of me.

I thought these feelings were love but it was never love. Or maybe it was on my side, just not the love I needed. These 'loves' were not what love should be, not nourishing, not good for the soul, just painful stabs of self-inflicted rejection. All those pre-teen emotions and fears of being unloveable and unwanted, of being wrong, came flooding back. It brought back the fucked-up, left-over emotions from Little Gay Me, popping up to say, 'HIIIII . . . JUST WANTED TO SAY, I KNOW YOU THINK YOU HAVE IT SORTED BUT YOU DON'T DESERVE LOVE. BE SAD PLEASE. SAD INSIDE. THANKS BYE!'

Hollywood had taught me that suffering was love. That yearning for someone and crying into your Frosties every morning listening to Smooth FM was in some way 'love'. If this was love, why was everyone so obsessed with it? It felt pretty shitty to me.

I needed a stern talking-to. Naturally it came from TV chef Andi Oliver.

Over the years in my kind of job you must meet thousands of people; some you see for work, some you merely email, some you host shows with from time to time, some you meet, welcome into your life and are then never without again. One of those people for me is Miquita Oliver. Smart, sharply funny and, like me, often single. We spent many an eve pouring our hearts out to one another about heartbreak and singledom. We were both very good for each other and very bad for each other, becoming a vacuum of whys and what-ifs about guys. 'What do you think THIS meant?' and 'Maybe if I write this, he will say this.' We got wasted on wine and wasted our time reading into the minutiae of boys' texts.

One day we found ourselves stuck when a French man kissed me. Sure, he was fit and kind to me and a great kisser. But also, very straight. Great. I was so confused. What did this mean? Was he actually a gay? Was he having a lol? Was I an experiment? Was it for attention? We didn't know. All we knew was that I now unfortunately had the feels. Miquita and I went round in circles on the whats and the whys of what this meant. But it was too deep, too emotional, too painful, too complicated and multi-layered. We needed the upper echelons of the Oliver family for this one.

I took a call from Miquita's mum, Andi. She is like the high priestess of advice and hot takes. She is also the definitive lover of oneself who we all try to emulate.

I explained my debacle and the fact that I had kissed a straight man and now I had the feels and how maybe, just maybe, this drunken kiss meant he was THE one . . .

'FOR-GET IT!' she said.

'What? Forget it?' I asked, 'But, he kissed me!'

'FORGET IT. No way!' she said.

But I couldn't forget it. I wanted to make it work … I think. 'But—' I tried.

'No buts. No. You deserve more. Tell you what we are not

going to do, we are not pinning our happiness on someone's drunken actions. NO.'

She told me off like never before.

'But—' I tried to argue again.

'FORGET IT! It's a waste of your time, your energy and of you. IF, and this is a big IF, if he comes knocking on your door and says I am ready to be gay and I want to take you on a date then sure, we will talk. Until then go out and be happy, be nice to yourself and then find someone who is ready to be obsessed with you. THAT is what you deserve. It's what we all deserve.'

A-fucking-men. I mean, you can't argue with that. I mean, I did try, but Andi was right. Enough.

I thought about what Andi had said. Why would I do this? On what planet would this make sense? I dived back into work, making that and me the priority. I was on prime-time radio by now and the eyes on the show meant there was this need to know more about my private life and specifically my love life. I'd cringe when asked in interviews, and laugh it off like 'hahahaha still single lol', crying inside.

I was never private about my private life on air, sharing all the ins and outs every day. As the listeners often did, I felt it only fair to share tales of my own family life and was happily mocked for being a single pringle for years by my team. But I began to dread chatting about relationships; everyone around me was beginning to settle down, their plus-one becoming their husband or wife.

My friends became accustomed to my lines of 'I'll never meet anyone, I'm gonna be single forever' and I'd think about maybe joining in a commune with some other singletons, or imagine living above the garage of my friends Aimee and Ian as their gay groundskeeper.

Aimee started her advice the way she started all her advice: 'The thing is . . .'

'. . . your job is very specific. Now, you need to concentrate on you and this show – when you're done it will be the time for a boyfriend, it will be a different chapter and you'll have more time for love after this,' she said.

Her words not only pacified me and let me plod on with my job but turned out to be precisely accurate. Almost to the day. Well, the day after to be exact.

I finished my final breakfast show on a sunny Thursday morning in August 2018 and by Friday I was in love.

Ending that show was like a giant exhalation of so many emotions, of childhood dreams coming true, of accomplishment, of love, pride, happiness, nostalgia, everything in one big emotional ball. There was only one thing for it: getting drunk with my team. We nearly ran down to the nearest Soho House, where we cracked open the espresso martinis and stayed boshing them back till close.

The next day it was Producer Fiona's birthday lunch at the inexplicably named Sexy Fish. But my hangover was biblical; I knew I had to be there but I couldn't. I don't know if you've ever drunk 3,000 espresso martinis and smoked 400 Marlboro Lights but I was not feeling very sexy nor up for fish. The Tube seemed too hot for this particular hangover and I couldn't handle the motion of a cab or a bus. I set off walking to Soho, where I was meeting her, looking green. She was lunching with a new DJ she was producing, Maya Jama, a supersonic radiant ball of Leo energy. She welcomed me with an 'OII-oiiii' and decided I needed a porn star martini. After four cocktails with flashing straws and light-up fish I was starting to get back in the room, and after a couple of lagers I was happily content with the day celebrating wonderful Fiona, and headed home.

When I got home I began to pack. After six years of early starts I had one more early rise, this time for a trip to the airport. It was to be the longest holiday I'd ever taken, three weeks to unpack what was my childhood dream come true and process the fallout from that. My door went. Miquita was there with a placcy bag full of Coronas, barging through while still on the phone and opening a bottle with her teeth.

'Errr what are you doing? Why aren't you ready? We're going out to Fiona's,' she said.

I explained that I'd done the early shift at lunch and wouldn't be going to the night-time pub bit as I was up early for my flight.

Miquita looked more confused than she had ever looked in her life. 'Sorry, you're going to bed early on the first Friday night of freedom in SIX YEARS? Why?' she asked.

'Well I have my flight at seven a.m. so I need to be there at five,' I replied.

'ARE YOU INSANE? WHY would YOU get up early EVER again?'

She did have a point.

I stopped packing and joined her at the kitchen table for a Corona. She began her pitch for the night ahead: 'OK. So. We go to Fiona's then you can come home. Just come with me so I'm not alone.'

OK, plan. It was only around the corner, I thought, I'd be back home before eleven.

And after an hour of blasting emo Annie Lennox songs and boshing bottles of Coronas I was primed and ready for round 2 of Fiona's birthday. We got to the pub and then the notion of a club was mentioned. A gay club.

'Oh nooo, I've got to get my flight still.' I checked my watch in a panic.

'Will you just cancel this bloody flight please?' Miquita was LIVID at my fixation on making this flight. After six years of being a slave to the alarm, I simply couldn't disobey the beeping beast of a clock next to my bed.

She asked that I accompany her now to the club, with the same promise that got me to the pub.

'Just come so I don't have to go in alone,' she said.

I love having my arm twisted, so agreed. 'OK FINE, let's go, ONE DRINK then I'm leaving.'

Reminder: I was nearly DYING of a hangover, was translucent, still hadn't showered, and wearing a below-average outfit, hastily put together in a hungover daze. I did not look OK hun. We got to the club on Hackney Road and were forced into those metal lanes of single human traffic so the bouncers could check our vitals. We got into the line and as Miquita went in, it was my time to have my ID checked – quite a quick process as I've always looked about forty-five. As I entered I looked across the entrance to the adjacent smoking area, where I laid eyes on someone I thought I knew. Wait, I know him, I thought. I stared over at this man in a beanie and tried to place him.

Now not to sound dramatic BUT . . . time did stop. Well of course it didn't, but it felt like that. Like when someone takes drugs in a Hollywood film, everything started to blur in slow-mo and everyone else lost focus as I walked past him, his image instantly ingrained on my memory forever. We stared at each other and did that confused I Think I Know You From Somewhere face.

With no time to register who it was, I was ushered in and met back up with Miquita. It was as packed as a gay club should be on a Friday, strobe lights flashing, smoke in the air, and over the banging music Miquita said . . .

'I just saw your husband outside.'

'Me too, the guy in the hat?' I asked. 'I think I know him from somewhere.'

'He is SO your husband, I can just tell,' she said.

'SHIT,' I said.

Fuck, I thought, this was NAHTTT the time to meet the love of your life. Not only was I looking like total shit, I was full of that post-partying paranoia and NOT in the mood for chatting to a stranger, just about managing to order a drink at the bar.

But Miquita was on one to make this happen and didn't waste any more time. Within ten minutes she barged over and introduced herself, probably bored of my twelve-plus years complaining that I didn't have a boyfriend and hoping this one would shut me up. Upon meeting she knocked his drink out of his hand and spilled it everywhere, then offered to buy him a new one and suggested we go outside to smoke. I followed them both sheepishly outside, checking my watch and worrying about this bloody flight in the morning.

'This is my friend, Nick, Nick, this is Meshach,' she said. 'Meshach is wearing suede, feel it,' she continued.

I stroked his shoulder with one finger in the least sexy way possible: 'Oh yeah. Suede. Great,' I said.

Meshach has these giant dark eyes that are full and kind and old beyond his years. These giant eyes looked right into me knowingly. Around the furore and the chaos of the club and the hangover and the drag queens arguing and the worry of the flight and the ending of a childhood dream he was instantly calming.

We started talking and we never stopped. We talked and talked until we noticed Miquita was no longer there. Not up to date with my ancient biblical names, I wasn't sure how to pronounce Meshach so avoided saying his name out loud and called him 'mate' for a few hours. We bonded over the fact that we were both in the same boat of being chronically hungover and had both been dragged to the club unwillingly by our mad friends. We sat at the bar drinking Red Stripes and told each other our dreams of what we both wanted to do with our lives, and by 6 a.m. the lights were on. So much for my one drink. We decided to go back to mine and drink some wine round the kitchen table. With the sun firmly sticking his head out to say hello, I realised my flight had left ten minutes ago.

I rebooked it for Saturday afternoon.

We spent the whole next day together, in that weirdly polite stage of newness where you do an impression of what you think the other person would like, insanely smiling, sitting upright and being courteous beyond belief. 'I'm fuckin' starving, I could eat a scabby horse' becomes 'Oh I'm slightly peckish, are you?'

'I feel like I am going to fucking die of hangover' becomes 'Might just open this window for some air.'

With both of us talking like we're in *Downton Abbey* and pretending we weren't dying of alcohol poisoning, we decided on some food and what we opted for still shocks me to the core. We decided to order THE worst hungover Deliveroo option known to man:

A

SALAD

FROM

PRET.

A salad on a hangover should be made illegal. This was the only time I saw Meshach order and eat a salad, FYI.

I never made that Saturday-afternoon flight. We watched *Batman Returns* and silently wished we'd not eaten a salad. I rescheduled for Saturday evening.

That one I didn't make either.

I'd never felt like this before; where usually I'd be a nervous wreck around someone I fancied, cringing at what was coming out of my mouth, I wanted to spend as much time with Meshach as possible and, as much as I craved the sunshine on my bones after that six-year slog of earlies, he was too important to leave. I eventually got there on Sunday evening at 9 p.m., four flights and thirty-six hours later than planned.

I spoke to Meshach every day while I was away. It was so easy, so right. All my thoughts of feeling wrong melted away and the hardness that I'd built around myself slowly softened again and I felt more me than ever.

I came home and went directly to dinner with Meshach. He was the antithesis to anything I'd ever felt before; where before I'd been nervous, now I felt truly content on dates with him, and we lol'd our way around east London bumping into various pals and wasting away our days getting to know each other. I was happy and fulfilled in a way I had never experienced before. It felt grounded and safe.

Before long that was it, we were just together.

Like the Sugababes when they wanted to exclude an annoying interviewer, we developed our own language.

I don't know when or why it started but now we begin our days by asking for 'some julies'. Being a julie means being loving; giving julies might be giving attention or giving a cuddle. One might need some julies if they've had a long day at work. We might ask if either of us feels 'julie-ish'. We'd declare, 'I'm julie-ish!' Or maybe complain that we don't have enough 'julies'.

It can't be taught and it can't be explained but, like the

subtlety of an eye movement, we know EXACTLY what we both mean. We don't know where this language came from or remember a time where we didn't use it. It wasn't a contrived plan to have our own dialect but it naturally evolved, like contemporary youth argot. I know Mesh is semi-cringed out by it but, like me, also wholeheartedly loves it. Objectively it doesn't mean anything, but to me, who feared he'd live a loveless life, it means absolutely everything. It's the absurdity of love, the joy of being free, and the comfort of that comes from being able to chat absolute shit in bed with your loved one. The deep-rooted security that comes with this level of closeness. It's a love language that melts away the horrid years of thinking I wasn't deserving of love, that I should be gay and sad forever. Now I'm free to roll around the bed chatting in tongues about absolutely nothing but with us understanding each other innately. I know what his sighs mean, what mood he is in from the speed at which he gets dressed, what songs he will want me to play next as we dance in the kitchen.

As a dancer Mesh's love language is touch; he has to touch, sometimes wrapping his entire body around mine, so we are in complete contact, with his feet going under mine like I'm wearing little human-foot high heels. On the couch he has to be touching; even if it's just a forearm or a toe, we are in constant contact. The problem is, it's a love language also adopted by my dog, Pig. She also HAS to make contact, so I have one on one side, one on the other, penned in by my needy loves. It's a contact I've never had before. As I sit here trying to type this book, unable to lift my arms, both constricted by love, I think about

Andi. What if I hadn't listened to Andi? What if I was still crying to Annie Lennox songs in the kitchen?

I'm saying this for all the self-doubters out there, the outsiders who beat themselves up, who have been taught they don't deserve to be loved. You do. If I can be in a healthy relationship, so can you. But it has to start with you loving yourself. Even if you can't do that yet, at least like yourself – you know you want to. Give yourself some julies.

7

That Bleedin' Dog Book

Imagine the scene. It's 1984 and Pete and Eileen are living the dream with their two kids and two cars on the drive. They are in their forties, having navigated through the complexities of raising their offspring; the labours of their time parenting are now to be harvested, as their little seeds have blossomed into interesting, funny humans. It's time for them to start having some adult time again, a time to leave the house without a shit-load of the stuff that babies demand on their rider. They can holiday in child-unfriendly places, go for dinner at 9 p.m. and get back to nights out with their mates again. Their lives have entered a new chapter. Not to say that kids aren't a blessing, but it must be a huge relief when they can wipe their own arse and make their own cereal. Imagine doing that EVERY DAY. I imagine being a parent is a bit like being a pop star's assistant: you get screamed at all day, you have to carry all their shit, facilitate their multiple outfit changes a day, mush up their food so they can swallow it down, comfort their daily breakdowns, and you're never thanked. But now Eileen and Pete had done it; the hard shift was over and the newfound peace that comes with middle age began to descend over them.

Then I came along: HIIIYAAAAA!

Like the film after the sequel, I was the third instalment no one ever wanted.

GRIMSHAW NUMBER 3: LOUDER, CAMPER AND MORE ANNOYING THAN EVER. COMING THIS SUMMER!

'Oh for fuck's sake.' I'm sure no one said this out loud (I hope) but I bet they thought it. They must've been gutted. What a rinse! Can you imagine? Not the sort of surprise Eileen, forty-one, and Pete, forty-three, were after as they faced binning off all the merits of being comfortable forty-somethings to be uncomfortable, tired forty-somethings and do all that baby nonsense again. I have visions of them praying to the patron saint of silence that I'd be a wallflower of a child or that I'd be born mute. No luck, I'm afraid. They knew I was trouble when poor Eileen tried to birth me; I couldn't keep still, wriggling all around and kicking her to pieces. Apologies, Mother! See I didn't *become* annoying, I was even jarring in the womb.

Out I came, and grew up feeling like there was little I longed for. All my juvenile wishes were granted – a packet of Iced Gems from time to time, some crisps after school, a quid for the ice cream van . . . childhood contentment fulfilled via snacks. When I wanted to show off they'd clap along as I did Cher shows and patiently watch along as I'd slip into Eileen's stilettos for yet another turn in the living room. Pete shaking his head at the madness of a gay drag show in his lounge by his eight-year-old son, while also trying to fight a smile as he was absolutely bloody loving the undeniably incredible show. We weren't a liberal art-farty household but I was free to decorate my room, play loud music constantly and to dance and scream around, and encouraged to spend time downstairs at grown-up dinner parties. They listened to my wishes for bikes and rollerblades, babysat my tamagotchi and engaged in the classic good behaviour = reward parenting style. I believe it's actually called bribery. But I knew they were on my side, that I, as my dad would say, 'went for nowt.' Translation: you're spoilt.

My parents had my back so much that they showed no sign of embarrassment when I insisted on wearing a probably semi-racist tea towel on my head during my obsessed-with-Ancient-Egypt phase. And when I say obsessed, I mean OBSESSED. It was an all-immersive Egyptian phase where I flooded my mind and bedroom with all things Cleopatra and co. I guess with feeling like an only child, plus my simmering gayness making me feel like an outsider, I had to create my own worlds. I had to create these spaces in my own head where I could indulge and be welcomed. And weirdly, one of those worlds was Ancient Egypt. I was hooked on mummification, the drama, the process, the effort of dragging someone's brains out of their nose with a hook before wrapping them in loads of scented rags. It fascinated me. It just sounded insane. I was so curious about other worlds, faraway lands and ancient practices, and although I wasn't allowed to mummify anyone, I was allowed to partake in some Ancient Egyptian practices of my own. I got bollocked for cutting a hole in a fitted sheet and wearing it over my head so it draped down to the floor. I'd found a fez in a joke shop and wore that on my head. I'd paint my eyes with Our Jane's Maybelline mascara and slip on my flip-flops from holiday while studying hieroglyph-ics and writing out my name as WATER REED FOLDED CLOTH BASKET.

Someone bought me a papyrus bookmark from Sharm el Sheikh for about £1.50 and I carried it delicately to my room, trapping it in one of Our Andrew's *Viz* magazines for protection and taking care of it like it was a priceless piece from the British Museum. I'd bring it down for show and tell for various aunties, who could look but NOT touch, as it was 'from Ancient Egypt' aka a factory in China. The peak of this phase was my camel. The camel was vital to the Ancient Egyptians; it had it all, like a Soho House on legs: food, milk, wool and travel, all wrapped up in one lumpy beast. So any Ancient Egyptian enthusiast needed one. Having not been allowed a real camel (fair), I was forced to create an imaginary one, which I'd lead around with my hand held up high behind me, tying him up out front after I'd walked him round the park. Imagine looking out of your window in 1990s Oldham and seeing a little fat kid draped in an M&S bed sheet and wearing a fez, with Julia Fox's eye make-up on, pretending to drag an imaginary camel around. I had no shame about it, and neither did my parents. They'd join in, holding the reins while I nipped for a wee in the park, hoisting up my bed sheet, looking back to make sure they were sticking to the rules of the game. They always were.

So I felt supported. I felt confident. I felt like I could get what I wanted, not in a spoilt way, because my requests were so uncomplicated and do-able, but my little wishes of snacks and attention were granted. And if I couldn't get what I wanted the first time, I could definitely wear them down. I don't know if it was a skill of debate or just pure annoyance but I would go on and on and on and on until Eileen cracked.

There was only ONE thing I couldn't convince them to do: let me have a dog.

Imaginary camel yes, real dog, no. I'd argue it was the same as walking the imaginary camel; the hard work is leaving the house, and we were doing that already with the camel so why couldn't we get a dog? But they wouldn't budge. My obsession with North Africa eventually sailed down the Nile, out of Egypt and across the sea, up the Thames, landing slap-bang in the middle of Battersea Dogs Home. The cats of Egypt were dead to me and now I was DOG MAD.

It was obvious life with dogs would be better. I was desperate for a furry pal, but Eileen was scared of them so we weren't allowed one. She'd shriek 'DOES HE BITE?' at an elderly brain-dead inbred cockapoo; it's not going to maul you to death, Mother. Rather than her go off for some sort of dog trauma release therapy, I was denied a canine companion and had to stroke random ones in the street to get my fix, chasing the odd golden retriever up the street for a petting.

I reckon I nearly got one, I think we were close and my way in was Dad. Pete liked dogs. He had one as a child and loved to talk about it. It was called Shep and was 'a proper dog', a black and white sheepdog living in inner-city Manchester. I'd ask Dad to tell me about Shep and he'd regale me with sweet tales of his times with Shep, mainly the dog biting his legs. It was probably experiencing some sort of sheep-less trauma, a working breed having to resort to rounding up the stray kids on the cobbled streets of Miles Platting. He'd rave about what a good dog it was, chasing the kids up and down the street, yapping at their ankles, thinking they were sheep. Sounds terrifying.

Whereas Eileen would shy away from dogs in the park, Pete would go over and give it the classic dad chat and pat them in a way only dads can, the dog trying to get away from this heavy-handed love. He'd confuse them with a horse and hard-pat them on the necks, nearly knocking them over.

As a kid my main dog interaction came from Auntie Carmel and Uncle Pete, neither of them my actual auntie or uncle btw, it was an unwritten rule that I just called them that. Unclear if it was enforced by me or them but it's one I still abide by to this day. They had a wonderful big black Labrador called Sandy. That was their family nickname, so it was like calling our dog Grimmy. I used to love going to their house for many reasons: Pete drank Stella and smoked, which I thought was v cool, they had a pulley light in the middle of their bed so when I'd sleep over I'd pull it and pull it and pull it, making the lights flash on and off, until I was moved into a spare room. But the main reason was Sandy. Although I was mad for a dog, my lack of time with them meant I was a little dubious about them and a little bit scared, if truth be told. Although Sandy was giant he was calm and gentle, flopping onto his side, where I'd full-body-hug him like one of those giant maternity pillows. I'd beg to sleep round at theirs for maximum dog time and once had him come stay at our house, which blew my tiny mind, running around screaming at the sight of a dog in the kitchen: 'AHAHAHAHHAAAAHHA LOOK AT HIM! WHAT'S HE DOING?? AHHAHAHA!! WHAT IS HE DOING??!!'

He was literally doing nothing.

A Labrador has the reputation that they can be something of a glutton, and Sandy was this sweeping generalisation come to life. He was a living, breathing dustbin, happy to eat everything and anything. Auntie Carmel and Uncle Pete used to run a newsagents and every so often he'd break out from behind the counter and scoff the nearest thing possible, knocking down a Snickers or two with his nose and eating them whole with the wrapper on. Respect, great choice. Or there was the time he broke into the stockroom and wolfed down forty-eight wrapped packets of Tunes. Bad choice. He had absolutely terrible explosive diarrhoea, but his nose was never bunged up ever again. His sinuses remained clear for all eternity.

Sandy was the first famous person I knew. It wasn't just us Grimmys and Sandys that were obsessed with his eating, Sandy actually became world famous for eating their Christmas dinner one year. He'd jumped up and scoffed the turkey, trimmings and potatoes, leaving the family with a Christmas dinner of carrots and a defrosted Sara Lee. News got out to a local paper and somehow – probably due to the lack of actual news – the story blew up and went worldwide. The TV channels and newspapers were loving this dog on a one-man mission to ruin everyone's day. Their house phone never stopped ringing; they were bombarded with requests for quotes for this funny, festive story with even *The Jay Leno Show* calling. For a short while Auntie

Carmel was like Oldham's Greta Garbo, crying out to the *New Zealand Times* that she wanted to be alone.

It was here that I experienced fame for the first time, Sandy cruelly tortured by the tabloids just for having a bit of turkey. He was body-shamed the world over; God let him live, we thought! After a short stay at the Priory his battles with turkey and gravy addiction settled for a while, until one day we had him come and stay.

It was the weekend of Our Jane's twenty-first and Eileen and Pete threw a party at our house for her, complete with an epic-sized, wedding-cake-style, iced birthday cake. Aware of the Crazed Christmas-Day-Ruining Savage, Eileen decided to move the giant cake to her bedroom – up the stairs, across the landing, around the bed and on top of a high dresser next to Pete's side of the bed. Safe there, she thought. She popped the lid on the box, closed the bedroom door tight and went down-stairs to welcome the guests.

Now this dog should have worked at airport customs because it smelt that cake, in a box, upstairs, in a room with the door closed, and went on the attack. Realising the dog was no longer present at the party, Eileen went on a search for him, franti-cally thinking he'd run out in the street or legged it back to Auntie Carmel's. Then she heard a crash. THAT BLOODY DOG! She ran up the stairs, tea towel on her shoulder flap-ping in the sheer velocity of a mum on a mission, and kicked open the bedroom door like Vin Diesel. There he was on the dresser, balancing on a side table with his face in the cake like Scarface about to party. 'SANDY. . .!' She got him in the nick of time. He'd only managed to have a few licks and seemed happy enough with that; he jumped down and rushed back to the party downstairs.

I thought this was the BEST thing I'd ever heard and it fuelled my desire for a dog – they're absolutely lol I thought, what legendary japes! Eileen wasn't as impressed and didn't tell anyone that a giant Labrador tongue had licked the cake, and just served it up to our guests. If you're reading this and were at that party, you may need a worming tablet. Please contact Eileen Grimshaw for more information.

The only other dog highs happened at school, whenever a dog got into the school playground. The place erupted like the cast of *Skins* all coming up on speed at the same time as 300 kids jumped on their chairs screaming and throwing their arms in the air at a stray Alsatian in the carpark. Like we were on safari, and we'd spotted a lion, we screamed and pointed and hysterically laughed as the teacher tried to calm us. They could never calm us after seeing a dog in the playground, like when you throw a blanket over a distressed parrot, we had to be plunged into darkness, with Miss having to draw the curtains and carry on the lesson in the dark.

I thought if I showed I was willing to look after a dog then I would win my parents over. Like I said, I had an innate skill to annoy them until I got my way. But the dog begging didn't work.

'Can we get a dog?'

'No.'

'What about a rescue dog? They need rescuing!'

'No way, they'll bite your hands off.'

'It would make me do more exercise.'

'Go on yer bleedin' bike we got you.'

'They can reduce cholesterol levels.'

'My cholesterol levels are fine thank you very much, my problem's me thyroid.'

'You know stroking a dog can make you happier?'

'Yeh but not when it's pissing and shitting everywhere.'

'I heard dogs can bring a family closer together.'

'No, we're close enough.'

'I think Gran would like it.'

'No she would not.'

I wouldn't let it go.

I don't know where it came from but one day I was handed a dog book, forever referred to thereafter by our family as 'THAT BLEEDIN' DOG BOOK!' said with a large exhale and rolling eyes. It was this little, travel-sized, pocket book with a smiling golden retriever on the front. To this day, it's the book I've read the most. While other kids were face down in *Goosebumps*, I was reading about the temperament of a Portuguese Water Spaniel and studying the exercise requirements for a Bernese Mountain Dog. The book had one page for each dog and on it hard stats, like Pokémon cards. The other boys at school were trading their football cards, Paul Scholes. Goals: 7. Caps: 11. Wins: 23. Height: 5'10.

I was like: Dalmatian. Likes: walks. Dislikes: cats. Height: 56–61 cm.

I put more work into studying this book than anything ever at school and before long I was fluent in dog. Clare Balding was shaking cos I not only had the same bowl haircut as her but totally could've stolen her job at Crufts. I took the book everywhere with me and drove Eileen and Pete mad with boredom, with them sighing heavily and casting saddened looks out the window every time I popped the book out of my pocket with a fact.

'Did you know that Bernese Mountain Dogs were used to rescue skiers?' I'd ask.

'Yes. Yes I did. You've mentioned that once or twice,' they'd say through gritted teeth.

I'd read it in bed, having my breakfast, on the way to school, with them having to prise it from my hands as I went through the school gates. I snuck it into Sunday trips to church, where I'd slide it into the hymn books to make out I was studying the lyrical breakdown of a banging hymn.

Until Eileen caught me and confiscated it into her bag – 'I thought you were quiet. Knew it was too good to be true! Dogs! In church!' she tutted. 'We could get one and call it Jesus,' I suggested.

I wore it out. The red ink had started to crack and flake, with the spine hanging on by a thread of gooey book string. The corners were folded in so I could locate at speed my favourite specimens. I ideally wanted a troupe of British Bulldogs, three to be exact, and I'd collect pictures of them and put them together in frames in my room as if they were my actual dogs. It was canine manifestation.

But it didn't work. After years of begging it was still a hard no from Eileen. Desperate to satisfy my pet needs, she tried to palm me off with various creatures who all turned out to have various ailments or personality disorders. I'd argue, 'We wouldn't have this with a dog.' We had the one-eyed hamster that we bought from the garden centre; I was beside myself that it had one eye and no one else would want it, nearly crying by the sawdust. Eileen caved and let me have it: *maybe this will ease the dog urges*. Turns out that there was no need to feel sorry for this one-eyed hamster as the reason it had one eye was probably that it loved fighting. It was the Mike Tyson of hamsters, running to attack you as you tried to drop some food in. After several attacks on me, my dad and Our Jane, I was shit-scared of it. Pete would have to get on his gardening gloves to get the wild bastard out of the cage and into its plastic exercise ball, where it'd run round the lounge carpet at about 35 mph. It was a lunatic.

Then we had the dwarf rabbit. I loved this cute little thing; he was friendly and tiny, perfect for my child-sized hands. One summer we went away and a friend looked after him. They didn't lock the cage and he escaped. Rather than break my eight-year-old heart they took a leaf out of *Esio Trot* and replaced him with a lookalikey rabbit. Same size, same vibe. Except this one wasn't a dwarf. It grew and grew and grew till it was too big for me to pick up. It was like a big ugly hare, not the cute baby dwarf I'd had. Our home went on to house a full menagerie – a budgie, fish, gerbils, sea monkeys, stick insects; you name it, I petted it. But nothing could quench my dog thirst. I was still reading the dog book, reciting the pros and cons of a Jack Russell to exhausted ears. I'd try to take the budgie out and play with it but it wasn't really interested and would just bash its head against the window trying to escape before shitting on the curtains. And the only thrill I got with the stick insects was putting them delicately in my sister's friends' hair when they weren't looking.

The dog pressure from me was sending Eileen over and one day she caved and I came home and she said, 'OK, OK – OK, for the love of God, you can have a . . . cat.'

A fucking cat? That's the opposite of a dog. Famously.

But I was happy to take what I could get and agreed a cat would be good. At least it was a pet that lived out of a cage who might cuddle me at night. We called him Floyd, as my brother wanted to call his kid Floyd and Eileen didn't like it so we ruined it by gazumping him via the cat. I loved Floyd. I created magical worlds and made stories up about him and christened him Floydus Dementus The Tap-Dancing Cat and would lift him by his arms, making him tap-dance as he bit my hands to be freed. Each night I'd drag him centre stage and raise him on his hind legs and tell the family the story of how he danced every night at the fictional theatre I created in my mind, 'Copper Faced Bills', based on the bungalow across the road, owned by a sweet old man called Bill. Here he would take to the stage alongside Smita Smitten The Showbiz Kitten, the French to his Saunders, and I'd swing him around and imagine him lip-syncing to some Frank Sinatra.

But cats are too cool for me. They just fuck off and come back whenever. I still craved the stupid neediness of a dog. I wanted it to be obsessed with me. I left home days after my eighteenth birthday, dogless, and now the dog dream was to be put on ice; freshers week is no place for a Rottweiler.

Once I moved to London, I was black-out drunk for a decade and could barely feed myself, so it felt wrong to inflict that onto a hound too. I was in and out, semi-nocturnal, and didn't fancy the RSPCA dragging my ass to the High Court for neglect, so decided it was best to wait it out.

Now that I have two dogs, Pig and Stinky Blob, who I deeply love, sometimes I understand Eileen's reluctance about being a dog owner, especially when you have a full-time job and three kids. Like I said, LOVE my dogs, but sometimes I am like PURLEASE leave me alone. Not so much Stinky Blob who, as the name suggests, is a blob; he's like having a pet rock. A smelly pet rock, as the name also suggests. Unclear why but he just stinks. He's a stinky blob, what can I say. Pig however is the problem child – she is Rue from *Euphoria*, non-stop whinging, a hellraiser on a one-man mission to chaos; she's beyond annoying, never not making a noise or a mess. She is a burly white Bull Terrier, one of those that looks pink in certain lights, and is called Pig because my neighbours had one as a kid and my mum was shit-scared of it.

'DON'T GO NEAR THAT PIG DOG!' she'd scream as I ran out to play. The late 80s and 90s: a time when dogs seemingly just ran wild on the Oldham streets.

I loved these 'pig dogs' though, with their weird big faces and tiny eyes, their square bodies making them the least aerodynamic of all animals. My Pig has no spatial awareness; she walks on your bare feet first thing in the morning, her tail beats against the bin like she's Nirvana-era Dave Grohl and she headbutts the bedroom door open in the morning when she wants feeding. She is a bitch. In all senses of the word. But I am obsessed with her. She is truly MAD. Like Naomi Campbell she has fronted a clothing campaign, is long and muscular, absolutely gorgeous, quite demanding, and was also discovered on Streatham High Street. Unlike Naomi Campbell, her farts are eye-wateringly vile.

I'd always wanted a pig dog. I remembered seeing them in the street at home and it filled me with dog-wanting nostalgia. They're weird like me, I thought. I'd heard that they were odd-balls and rumours that they did weird things due to their eyes being so far apart that if they get into a corner, they get stuck. Their eyes are so close to the walls that they think they're in a box. I was sold.

I met Pig for a speed date at Battersea Dogs Home and then a few days later, when we were both happy with each other, I went to bring her home. By pure coincidence, on this day I was lent a car by Mercedes for a week or so. It was a bright red obnoxious two-seater convertible and I was worried they would stop me getting her, as it wasn't the most traditionally dog-appropriate automobile. I tentatively opened the passenger door for Pig, thinking she might not easily take to me, but she instantly hopped in and got comfy. She may as well have put sunglasses on. I walked around and got in next to her. It was a glorious day and I thought, you know what, let's take the roof off. She clocked the roof descending and looked me in my eyes with such contentment – as Jane from Battersea said, 'Oooooh it's like she's won the lottery!' I fired up the V12 engine and we drove over Battersea Bridge in the sunshine like a far less suicidal Thelma and Louise.

A few days later everyone came to visit, and marvelled at her noisiness, general craziness and wild levels of energy. I struggled with this new flatmate at first. 'Wow she's exhausting! She wants constant affection and validation. And she doesn't shut up, she's always making a noise,' I said.

My friend Aimee had some thoughts. 'Now you know how we feel – it's the dog you deserve. She is literally you.'

Wow. She is. Noisy, annoying, insatiable, but loving and sometimes misunderstood.

My Dad's intense level of petting continued when he met Pig. 'GOOD LAD GOOD LAD,' he'd say when giving Pig one of his shiatsu-level pattings. 'It's a girl, Dad,' I'd say. 'He dunt mind, he, she, whatever, GOOD LAAAAD,' he'd continue. You'd experience the same level of dog-patting pressure when he applied suncream for you. 'You're not cleaning the car!' Eileen would yelp in pain as he whacked on the SPF like boot polish. Dad liked them coming up from London to visit; they'd jump out the car and go apeshit in the garden after four hours in the boot. He didn't like them on the couch – he barely liked us on the couch. 'If you're tired GET TO BED,' would be his stirring words waking you from your post-school nap. Bed? It's 4.15 p.m. So dogs were a no-go. They were to remain at ground level, downstairs, preferably silent and not moving in their bed.

Then Stinky came along, who – unlike me for Eileen and Pete – is an absolute angel of another addition to the family.

Unlike me he is silent, content and very happy on his own. Like me, he is occasionally smelly, snoozy and frequently overweight.

Stinky causes me no problems, whereas with Pig I spend my life trying to wrestle things out of her mouth in the street – an old banana skin, a stray glove or sometimes a rock. Please note, I'm not saying pebble, I'm saying ROCK. Imagine eating a rock, swallowing it down in one. One Christmas Eve in Oldham when I was out last-minute shopping, Eileen called in a panic: 'Pig has been sick . . . and it's just . . . rocks.'

'ROCKS?' Me thinking Eileen's mixed up her HRTs and lost it.

'I'm serious, not stones, rocks. I could hear gagging but it wasn't sick that came up. It was loud, really loud. Like someone throwing ten rocks on the floor.'

'What?!' I ran home to check on her. Worried I'd find a dead dog.

When I got there she was happy as anything, running around the garden trying to rip a branch off a tree. I tempted her with some food to see if she'd eat and she inhaled it and went back out to destroy some more nature. I thought I'd take her to the vets JUST in case. After an X-ray they found a few more rocks inside her. Twelve to be exact. TWELVE! So before puking up the ten, this mental case had been happily running around with TWENTY-TWO rocks inside her. She'd eaten a rockery. Anyway, £6,300 later and they were out of her. She did it again six weeks later, this time only eating four but still having to have the op. Maybe don't eat rocks?

I actually have a full census of questions for these beloved hounds who, try as I might, can never answer:

1. Can you just NOT roll in muddy puddles?
2. And if you do, can you just bath yourself?
3. And why are you happy being wet in a shitty puddle but cry in a nice, warm bath like it's torture?
4. Ever thought about not sleeping all day and then walking around with your noisy toenails all night? Maybe save the snoozes for night-time?
5. Why do you come over to me to fart? Is that a cry for help?
6. You know fetch would be easier if you let me throw it?
7. What's with the volume of barking at the door? What hell do you think we are about to experience?
8. Why must you vomit EXCLUSIVELY on the edge of a rug? You can see the rug, as you both choose to do it on the corner of it, so why not just do it on the tiled floor below?

Maybe Eileen was right after all, dogs are a pain in the arse.

But as I sit here and write, they wiggle their tails, staring me out, desperate for my attention, and it makes me forget all the annoyances and invite them up for a cuddle. We do have this in common though. We all just need to be constantly stroked, adored and fed. Is that too much to ask?

We spend the days together with Mesh in a perfect foursome, occasionally dreaming of a third dog. Just like Eileen and Pete would back in the 80s, pre-me. 'Would three be too much?' I ask Eileen. 'Three is crazy. Never have three,' she says.

8

Hardcore Ecstasy

No offence to my dad but 'lying around watching music videos and getting pissed up with your mates' did ACTUALLY get me very far. The hard-working sensibilities knocked into my dad by his childhood in the Victorian slums of Manchester meant he was outraged by a lot of modern life. His kids' disdain for the church, authority and Johnny Mathis, teamed with their love of lager and banging house music, meant that we weren't always reading from the same page. During school he was enraged that I wasn't gagging to run home to do homework but instead was watching Missy Elliott videos and cranking *The Fat Of The Land* up to full volume at teatime.

'Yer mother does not want to hear about someone smacking a bitch up while she's gettin' tea ready!' he'd scream up the stairs.

Our Clare, my cousin, took me one Friday to see The Prodigy live in concert and I was never the same again; music couldn't be loud enough or mad enough. It was a baptism of fire and it triggered something inside of me. I wanted to be Keith Flint. Then my mum took me to M People, so I also wanted to be Heather Small. I think I have successfully found the happy medium between the two.

At home I was allowed to play my music loudly and dance around my bedroom but it wasn't all dance parties and The Prodigy gigs. The notion of having to have a 'proper job' lay heavy over us, not in a scary militant way, more in a (very aggressive) encouraging way. Reports, school and future career plans were top priorities for Dad and anything else was a distraction. Whereas my priorities, obviously, were the polar opposite. I was lost in a daydream of what he called nonsense. My dad didn't get it. He saw music as a frivolous luxury that I didn't need, whereas to me it was the only thing that mattered. He'd be listing off career options like a doctor, a lawyer, an accountant, as I smiled and nodded while daydreaming of a life lost in a sea of So Solid Crew and inflatable furniture.

'Your Jane got top marks in her O levels, what do you think you'll get?' he'd say, still calling GCSE's by their old name.

'I wont get any O levels cos they've not been called that for about twenty years,' I'd reply, cracking myself up from the dining room revision camp.

'Ya bleedin' smartarse . . . you know what I mean, that's your bleedin' problem, you don't take anything seriously,' he'd shout back.

Well, no, cos I'm fifteen.

Off he'd go and leave me to my own devices for revision. I just couldn't do it. I didn't care and try as I might, nothing was going in. I almost wanted to fail so I could do what I wanted. Rather than attempt to learn anything I'd paint my nails with pens and pretend I was hosting the Brit Awards, before reading about All Saints having a big one at the Met Bar in SKY Magazine. Can't

I just do that? That seems so fun, I'd think. Much more fun than the periodic table. While Pete was encouraging me to work hard to get a proper job, Jane and Andrew had already fallen for that trick and, through experience, actively encouraged me to do the opposite.

'WHATEVER YOU DO DONT GET A PROPER JOB.' Jane grabbed me sternly by the shoulders and looked deep into me.

Her SAVE YOURSELF screams rang loudly and it felt like she'd sacrificed her soul for my future. They'd run the school gauntlet and when they noticed my knack for chatting absolute breeze and my inability to revise, they suggested I swerve the bar exams.

They were also the perfect tutors in music; they knew what slapped and what didn't and the house was a constant argument over the level of music pumping from our bedrooms. Andrew was my most passionate teacher, playing me De La Soul's *Three Feet High and Rising*, the Beastie Boys' *Licensed To Ill*, N.W.A.'s *Straight Outta Compton*, Public Enemy, New Order and Kraftwerk. Our Jane got me into the sexiness of Michael Hutchence as we learnt the lyrics to INXS songs, A Guy Called Gerald's 'Voodoo Ray' and Soul II Soul's 'Back to Life'. It felt like that song rang out over the suburban gardens of our area for eternity as I jumped in and out of Pete's sprinkler screaming.

They played Dee-lite, A Tribe Called Quest, Happy Mondays and the KLF; we borrowed Dad's company car to drive around in, singing our hearts out while seat-dancing along to 'Last Night A DJ Saved My Life' and Prince's '1999'.

Andrew's room was where it was at though. He had a down-stairs bedroom, a room that managed to look more 80s than Ferris Bueller's. A red metal half-moon headboard with red metal blinds to match teamed with a graphic, monochrome duvet cover. His metal shelves adorned with Joop! aftershave and a grey soap version of a Porsche 911. He had an anti-Thatcher comic book about the Falklands War, *Viz* magazine, CDs, vinyls and magazines neatly piled everywhere. His room felt like he'd MADE IT, it felt so cool to little me, like the VIP section of the house, elevated cos I was never allowed in it. He had (and still has) discerning taste in music, 99 per cent of anything he saw on TV or heard on radio back in those days was 'absolute shite', a phrase he still uses for most of the music of today. He made me realise the difference between good and bad, real and perform-ative, creative and lazy. His teachings meant I searched out the different, the alternative, the exciting, and I leant towards the noisier end of the spectrum, shying away from the mainstream unless it was truly top-notch.

There were times where we'd take family trips to a gig; we'd team up with Auntie Carmel's family and off we'd go en masse to see the Brand New Heavies, Carleen Anderson and M People. We'd pile into the back of Auntie Carmel's minivan and if you were lucky you could sit on a wheel arch, if not just enjoy the ride and roll around the metal box for a while before descending on the Apollo for some 'Midnight At The Oasis' action. All these moments made music so important to me; it was how we had fun, what shaped the days and shifted the moods of the house.

I was totally wound up by the feel of music, magnetised to the thrill of the noise, lost in the lyrics, happily dancing around to banging house music in Andrew's room and listening intently to the emotions of Ella Fitzgerald from the dining room courtesy of Dad. I couldn't have a moment of silence.

Dad's taste was different to the rest of the house. He wasn't feeling N.W.A. He was however very much feeling Ella, Frank Sinatra, Barbra Streisand, Bob Marley and Bill Withers. He had about six CDs that were just on repeat from about 1985 to death. He liked what he liked and that was that, like his clothes, he kept it simple and classic. He liked music, of course, but his world was far from dictated by it like mine was, and he was less than overjoyed at the concept of me wanting a career in music.

Pete was born poor. He lived in prefab housing that was anything but fab, thrown up post-war to house the needy like Gran Beattie and her two kids. These humble beginnings rooted him as a man of integrity, a man who wanted to work hard, a man who had pride in what he wore, how he sat – every element of his being he had a sense of pride in because he'd grafted for it.

So when he'd made a few quid and had a house over his wife and kids' heads, the last thing he wanted was me ripping up my clothes, blasting out punk and aggressive rap records, wanting to sack off education to work in music. Maybe I'd be a singer? Maybe a rock star? Maybe I'd be like Keith Flint? Better learn an instrument, I thought.

Pete enjoyed a brass band, so he encouraged me to join the school brass band, which seemed pretty cool at primary school and soul-crushingly naff at secondary school. We'd play a night or two a week after school and as much as I loved music, I hated this! Too many rules and some boring song I'd never heard of. I'd only agreed to join cos I wanted a saxophone to follow my loves the Brand New Heavies, but I was instead handed a trumpet and told the sax was a woodwind instrument and this was a brass band.

I loved the word 'band' but hated the word 'brass', it just didn't seem unruly enough, so I'd do anything I could to be thrown out. I'd purposely play a bad note or chat to someone next to me in an attempt to be sent home early. I also had a real problem with the smell of the wet metal. 'WELL DON'T SMELL IT THEN,' the teacher would shout at me weekly, overhearing my complaints. We'd gather in the school hall to blow our respective horns; some kids had massive tubas to drag around, others the always-hilarious trombone, and after being lumped with a trumpet I was later demoted to a crappy cornet. Always hated that word. 'Cornet'.

I never knew what the hell was going on, and just opted to blow a random C or an F when I felt like it. 'I'm more freestyle,' I'd say to my parents when they'd pressure me into practice, 'I don't perform well unless I'm with the full band.' My lack of practice meant I'd get kicked out of the band near weekly, with my mum calling and begging them to let me back in, probably to keep my annoying self away from her for one more hour a week. Thursdays we'd go to the music centre in Oldham where all the trumpet-blowers, trombone-pumpers and tuba-luggers from schools across Oldham would combine and form one massive nerd machine of brass. This was easier for me as there was what felt like hundreds of people there to disguise my infernal tootings. There was also a vending machine, which became the highlight of my week.

As well as that I tried the choir, where each week I was pushed a row back, then another, then another, then another until before long I was just standing outside in the car park singing to myself. I'd go home and attempt to write emo lyrics with the guitar Our Andrew had bought me; I'd sing it back, trying to find my voice or any sort of melody. I could never find it. The lyrics, melody and my voice all had one thing in common: they were shite. I started to rethink the rock-star career route.

I did love singing, even thought it sounded somehow even flatter than my speaking voice. My optimum singing experience would be in Dad's car. We'd go on car trips with the same Simon & Garfunkel tape going over and over, all singing along to 'The Sound Of Silence', a morbid-toned death choir in the company car: 'Hello darkness my old friend,' staring out of the window as we went for a 'ride out'. Dad loved a ride out as a chance to listen to music and we'd do it on a Sunday mostly. 'I AM A ROCK! I AM AN ISLANDDDDDDDDDD!' I'd sing in the back with my bowl-cut hair rocking, playing third wheel in the car.

I remember wholeheartedly enjoying these moments but longing for something cooler. Sure, I enjoyed the Ride Out

Sing-A-Long Sessions, but I started to tire of the repetitiveness of them on an endless cycle. Pete had a six-disc CD changer in the boot, the height of luxury back in the day. Before your journey you'd pre-empt what kind of drive you fancied as you picked from the Ikea CD tower in the house. 'Oooh what shall we have? Bit of Tina? Barbra Streisland?' For some reason my dad could not say Streisand. He liked to add an L in there to make it sound like her own theme park. Only one of the most famous people of his era or ever and he STILL couldn't get her name right, so I couldn't take offence when he got my name wrong for 90 per cent of my life.

'Andrew, ANDREW, ANDREWWWW CAN YOU HEAR ME?' he'd shout.

Erm, I'm called Nick.

'You knew what I bleedin' meant.'

We'd load up the six-stack CD player and away we'd go, Simon & Garfunkel first, followed by *Tina Turner's Greatest Hits*. I'd stare out of the misty back window and imagine music videos. In my head I'd slip inside Tina's high heels and low-denier tights and imagine the sheep upon the hill we were whizzing past were my adoring crowd, throwing my seven-year-old head back and forth and lip syncing to 'Nutbush City Limits': 'CHURCH HOUSE GIN HOUSE' as I waved my arms around in joy.

I'm obsessed with the thought of us speeding through a country lane in the Yorkshire Dales, with my parents in a company car blasting 'Steamy Windows' by Tina Turner on a Sunday afternoon. Absolutely unaware that I was singing along with my middle-aged parents to a song about Tina Turner having sex so aerobic it's causing the windows to become opaque through the sheer steam being produced by her body heat. 'Love this one!' I'd shout over the music. But I was hungry for my own sounds.

Every now and then we'd venture into Rochdale for a shop. There'd be a few places I'd be desperate to hit, namely Woolworths for pick 'n' mix and HMV for a 'nosey'. The high street was built up a hill and halfway up what seemed a very steep incline, we'd have a pit stop for the potato man. The potato man sold hot new potatoes in a paper bag, smothered in butter and engulfed in tons of salt. We'd scoff them down in the street, too hot for your hands but just right for your mouth. Once dehydrated from our week's-worth of salt in one snack, we'd split up: Mum in M&S, Jane in River Island and me off to HMV. I'd flick through the racks, taking note of the genres and studying the artwork; Madonna's *The Immaculate Collection*, Sinéad O'Connor's *I Do Not Want What I Haven't Got*, Sonic Youth's *Goo*, Massive Attack's *Blue Lines*, *Screamadelica* by Primal Scream. Eileen's disapproving face curled up in shock at me wanting an album called *Doggystyle*. But one day after a season of good behaviour, Eileen let me have a tape.

'I'll take this please,' I said.

After an hour of looking I'd settled on the one, the album that would be my first taste of my own music. After years of happily passively listening to Tina and Barbra, I was to make a choice of my own. I went for a double tape cassette compilation. I'd listened to it in-store to check I liked it and was sold on track one alone.

Eileen looked worried. 'Are you sure you want this one?' she asked with a Marge Simpson grumble. 'Do you think this is appropriate for him, Jane?'

Jane shrugged her shoulders and carried on looking around.

'I don't know if I like the sound of that . . . is it for kids?' she continued.

'Please Mum! There's no parents sticker on it, so it must be for kids, pleeeassseeee I love it,' I begged.

'I don't know about this one. What about something else?'

'Noooooo. Pleeeeease . . . I looooooove iiiiit!' I begged, now on my knees in HMV Rochdale.

'OK, OK, OK. Let's get it. But you have to behave the rest of the weekend.'

Unbeknown to her at the time, Eileen had agreed to buy me an album that would create and cement my love for the sesh deep within me. She had set me off on one. I was not even eight and she'd unwillingly bought me a collection of house and rave bangers wonderfully titled *Hardcore Ecstasy*.

I walked back down the hill to the car clutching my new prized possession like my life depended on it. As we got closer to the car park the realisation that I was to be in charge of the music on the way home for the very first time set in and I started to run with excitement.

I got in and ejected Our Jane's INXS tape and got ready for some serious *Hardcore Ecstasy*. The sound of searing synths filled the car and as I rolled down the window, the sweet sound of Rozalla's 'Everybody's Free' began to blast around the Pay & Display precinct. I didn't know at the time why I felt so emancipated, but I felt those first words of freedom like a breath of fresh air. Maybe I'd had a previous life of persecution, because I FELT those words. The emotive start, the build, the impending sense of coming up, the anticipation in the air as her vocals about being free belted out as my bowl cut blew in the wind all the way back home.

'EVERYBODY'S FREE TO FEEL GOOD!' I sang high and mighty: 'THIS IS BRILLANT, MUM!!' as I raved around the back seat, both arms in the air.

The looping piano rose and rose, taking me to another level of happiness as I slapped the plastic sides of Mum's Fiesta as the synths stabbed serotonin right through me. WOW, I thought when it ended, Rozalla is so right! Everybody is free to feel good! WOW! Next up was Oceanic's 'Insanity', a ravey tune about being taken to a place of no return, to a place of insanity. God bless Eileen for granting my wishes in buying it for me, but this tape was the worst thing you could play to a hyperactive kid; it sent me over the edge. Sound-wise it was nearing happy hardcore with its synthetic dance feel; it had crowd noises, which I'd rewind and listen to over and over. I was entering deadly levels of being gassed up by rave bangers.

Once home I took the tape upstairs and danced around to Brothers In Rhythm, Sabrina Johnston, Bizarre Inc, a collection of songs all about being in a state of ecstasy. All the while not having a clue why everyone in 1991 was so intent on being SO happy they actually felt ecstatic. I didn't overthink it. Off I'd go like a pilled-up Billy Elliot, dancing around the house to the uplifting joyfulness of these songs, letting it run to the end then flipping it over for the other side.

Eileen really put the dance inside of me and it never left. The layers of piano loops, handclaps, soulful vocals, the rattle of the cowbell had me hooked and I'd crank it to full blast, throwing my head around, giving myself self-induced whiplash. Occasionally Our Andrew or Jane would burst in with a 'woiiii oiiiiiiii!' and a wolf-whistle and dance around with me. I treasured this tape, taking it downstairs and trying to get Gran Beattie on board with the dance classics. I'd take it in the car on trips out with Mum, pulling up at the big Asda with 'Charly' by The Prodigy reverberating through the windows.

I became obsessed with clubbing. I'd never been, obviously, or even seen a club with my very own eyes. But it was in our lives, it was part of the fabric of Manchester at the time. I'd spend my days out in town collecting flyers for all the clubs, telling Mum and Dad, 'I want to hand out flyers as my job when I'm older.' Silence. When Jane went to university she'd post me flyers for Cream and Essential and I'd carefully adorn my walls with them and all the ones I'd collected so my room looked like the green room of some dirty club. I'd drag Gran Beattie up the stairs to show her them all: 'This one is a rave in Leeds, this one is a club in Glasgow and this one is aaaalll night and it's so fun that it goes on all the next day too, look!' She'd oooh and ahhh at these little postcard-like bits of cardboard adorned in pills and smiley faces: 'Ooooh they're lovely, Nick.'

I'd crank up *Hardcore Ecstasy* one more time as Gran Beattie evacuated, fingers in ears. I'd press my ears right next to the speaker, hearing every pop of my budget tape player. It put a smile on my face like nothing else and the album was all I listened to for about two years straight, wearing it out til the white writing had faded off the sides. I don't know if I was born this way or the tape instilled it in me but I realised I was a raver. It just felt so right and as I grew and dipped in and out of trends, obsessions and fashions, the one thing I stayed true to was house music. It never fails to make me happy, be it the nostalgia of that tape or the rousing power of the music.

Dopamine and euphoria are a heady mix to a seven-year-old and the rewarding combination of synthetic beats and dancing led to ecstatic levels of happiness, so house music and (as I grew older) clubbing became my medicine. As that seven-year-old on the way home from Rochdale I liked the noise of it all but ten years later as a club-going seventeen-year-old it took on another purpose. It was the therapy I needed to free the angst formed in my teenage self-hating years, and I found solace on the sweaty club floors, dancing with strangers as if my life depended on it. Sometimes it did. These electronic songs that had been planted in my head via the HMV Rochdale took on another job once I went clubbing. They healed me, taking on a near-religious quality, needing, like church, to be revisited on a weekly basis.

To Eileen and Pete, *Hardcore Ecstasy* was a collection of 'bloody awful' songs all about 'bloody idiots' being off their heads. I mean sure, maybe. But they were more than that. To me they were all about making it, about being free, about expression and relief. Songs discovered in the innocence of childhood when life IS free and hopeful. Little did I know how essential they'd be to me once I became an adult. They sang about joining hands, coming together as one and reaching the promised land. 'It's bloody rubbish,' Pete said.

Electronic music moved me in a way I couldn't communicate to Pete. I compared it to his love of United. He had football, I had *Hardcore Ecstasy*.

'Don't be so bleedin' stupid,' he said.

9

We Like, We Like to Party

I felt constantly out of place as a kid. At school, in class, on lunch breaks, even on trips to the football with my dad, I was always very aware of myself. Aware that I felt different and not comfortable in my own skin, my awkward growing limbs getting in the way all the time. Sometimes, I felt like I didn't fit in at home either. There was a big age gap between me, Jane and Andrew – eleven years and thirteen years respectively.

'That. Is. Disgusting,' Jane said to my mum on hearing the news that I was on the way. Thankfully, she grew to like me.

The age gap meant I kind of grew up like an only child, by the time my memory kicked in, Andrew was a behemoth of a man to little me and Jane a fully functional adult too. So I was often out of the loop on things; they'd reminisce about the 70s and trips to Texas to see family, before a chorus of 'You wouldn't remember, it was before you were born.'

This sounds like they just sat around excluding me – quite the opposite. I never felt unloved, I wasn't held against my will to hear warm family stories of life before me, they showered love upon me. But I wasn't like Andrew and I wasn't like Jane. Looking back they seemed to be annoyingly perfect, actually impossible to live up to.

Firstly, I wasn't as clever as Andrew or Jane, their school exam results etched into my mind by my ever-encouraging father.

'Jane got GREAT results you know. And Andrew!' he'd say through gritted teeth.

'Oh I know,' I'd reply, nervously attempting to revise in the dining room.

Jane and Andrew just seemed to GET IT. The looks, the humour, the charm, the brains. Andrew educated me on the importance of trainer brands and Jane taught me (with success) the power of Mariah Carey's 'Fantasy', and attempted to do the same with maths, with less successful results. Looking at numbers was like someone speaking in Japanese to me. And still is. 'WHY DON'T YOU GET IT?' she'd ask in frustration, helping me with percentages.

Not only were they dead clever, they were popular too. They were funny, quick and good-looking. Jane was gorgeous, with this giant tooth-filled smile across her face, always make-up-free with perfect skin, her dark brown eyes twinkling as she smiled, with hair to her waist, in a vest like she was off to a CK One campaign.

'She looks like Jane!' I'd say to Mum and Dad as we watched *Pretty Woman*.

'Yes, erm, yes,' they'd say. Half agreeing, half crying inside that their daughter looked like a prostitute walking up Hollywood Boulevard.

I idolised her and thought saying that she looked like Julia Roberts was the biggest compliment I could bestow on any living human. Still true tbf.

She seemed to effortlessly breeze through school with straight A's and cool friends. Our Andrew was the same, if not slightly more adored, by family and friends alike. He was tall and skinny, with a sharp James Dean jawline, 6 foot 3 with a hard coolness impossible to impersonate. He had that perfect mix of very handsome but also absolutely handy in a fight at the football. And he's still got it. He's in his fifties now, and a whole array of my friends still declare their love for him on a regular basis.

'Your Andrew is gorgeous.'

'Not being funny but your brother is well fit you know.'

'Lol if I was your sister-in-law. Actually, I wouldn't be loling if I were with Andrew, I'd take it very seriously. He's a real man.'

Enough.

Enough praise to make you want to vomit, and things said that no one should ever hear about their own brother.

They're obsessed. And rightly so.

Just like the female Andrew Grimshaw fans, I was obsessed with both of them. They'd breeze in and out of the house in their leather jackets, Andrew's sharp and tailored like 90s Prada, Jane's oversized and a little more grungy.

I loved their tenacity for night-time, seeing them leave Friday 7 p.m. only to return with sweat-soaked dungarees stinking of fags at 9 a.m.; it stirred my soul. My imagination went wild choreographing the 'rave' in my brain. Clubbing just felt like a rite of passage, written in the stars, something I had to do. Andrew would play me 808 State and A Guy Called Gerald and it was like taking that first drag of a cigarette, the exhale just hitting me right. It wasn't just the music, it was everything: their outfits, their funny stories, the flyers they'd bring home, the lighters I'd find in their denim jacket pockets – all this magical paraphernalia planted a seed in my head, and sparked a love affair with the idea of after-hours. I just thought they were the coolest people on Earth.

And I the uncoolest. While they were long and slender, I was round and short. While they aced school, I might as well have been sitting in my dunce cap facing the wall. And while they loved sport and were adored by the popular kids, I was playing my tamagotchi solo and going to Simply Red gigs with Mum and her friends.

While it was their academic skills that Dad adored, I was lovingly gazing at them for another reason, something I was mystified by at the time: their love for the sesh. While I was home for a weekend with the olds watching *Noel's House Party*, they were off to a rave. I didn't even know what a 'rave' was back then but whatever they were up to, I wanted in. They seemed to be really good at it and were REALLY happy whenever they came home from one.

It was the mid-90s and I was gagging to be older, to be a part of something I could feel was happening outside of suburbia. The telly was saying things like 'Cool Britannia', a name given to the glory days of the abundant 90s, with Young British Artists like Damien Hirst and Tracey Emin confusing the oldies. They partied with Noel Gallagher and Naomi Campbell and I saw these lot as the superhero versions of Andrew and Jane. Like them but souped up on acid. Literally! No, not literally. I remember seeing the chaos of London nights out in the paper and Pete and Eileen shaking their heads at these pissed-up celebrities being celebrated.

'Bloody state of them!' Pete would say, flicking through his *Daily Mail*.

But I loved it, fell for it hook, line and sinker – I was like 'Yeahhhhh, cool Britain go!' For someone like me, bored in Oldham, unable to rage like Andrew and Jane, being decidedly average at school and feeling generally lost, it was like a postcard from another planet. One I needed to fly to.

My frustrations at not being able to go out as a kid drove me mad. I thought it was boring round our way, all bungalows and beige, I thought everything was boring, Britain was boring, food was boring, the telly was boring, not very *COOOOL* Britannia round here, I thought. I complained it should be called just Cool London. My boredom spurred me on to set my sights on the capital for the first time; I was hypnotised by the boozy decadence going on in that there London, sucked into the reckless pop culture scenes of the 90s.

Stuck in suburbia as a bit of a billy-no-mates, I lusted after this hedonistic way of life through pissed-up Gallagher brothers, Goldie, and Scary Spice falling out of the Met Bar. It looked ideal.

Today the kids idolise Pilates-loving Kendall Jenner and relish the familiarity of Molly-Mae vlogging us through her new line of nude pyjama bottoms, but my childhood icons were – well, basically hellraisers. Back then basicness wasn't aspirational; I needed a level of distinction between my suburban life and celebrities – I wanted nutters! I wanted Grace Jones, Keith Flint and Madonna at her 90s c*nty best!

Even though I wasn't old enough to go out, all roads led to the weekend. Fridays were all about *TFI Friday* for me. I'd be allowed a chippy for tea – chip muffin please with enough vinegar to make you cough – and I'd get to sit in the lounge solo and watch Chris Evans live and loose in a pub. I definitely wasn't the target audience and definitely missed the punchlines of the gags, but the energy of the studio had me hooked. I loved the mess, the lager sloshing on the floor as Shaun Ryder came on and waffled some madness before a band crowd-surfed downstairs. After that I'd stay up late to watch *The Word* and *Eurotrash* and shriek in shock at the wonderful female hedonism of *The Girlie Show*. Come Saturday I'd wake and flick through *The Face*, idolising smokers, painfully thin gawky models and pissed-up obnoxious celebrities, a menagerie of party extremists screaming 'Firestarter', here to make the noise. A noise I really liked the sound of.

At college we tuned in to the radio to idolise the boozy days of Sara Cox, out all night and hungover on air. While Eileen would tut in disgust at her ad-hoc observations and ravey selections on the school run, it was *EXACTLY* what I needed to hear, revving me up for another day at school. I remember gasping in amazement at seeing Zoe Ball swigging a bottle of whisky on her wedding day in a cowboy hat.

'Legends! I should do that!' I thought.

Idiots!

It was the perfect cocktail: me a queer kid in suburbia, feeling like an outsider with the party-professional siblings, daydreaming in a time of burgeoning partying Britain. But being ten years old, all I could do was dream of the future. I didn't want to be the outsider forever; if this suburban life wasn't to work for me, something else must. I craved the bedlam.

I spent my early teen years longing to go clubbing, hearing tales from my siblings making me sick with jealousy over something I'd never experienced. I wanted to be one of those 24-hour party people; I couldn't wait to go out and get fucked up, and by fourteen I was chomping at the bit of alcohol excess.

I'd beg Eileen to pick me up *Vice* magazine on her way home from work.

'VICE? Oh I don't like the sound of that,' she'd say. 'Is it meant for kids?'

'Yeah yeah, just get it,' I'd say, then wait for her to bring it home like some biblical text I 'needed'.

I'd sit on my transparent inflatable armchair in my room blasting out 'Cigarettes & Alcohol' and deep-dive into the glorious editorials on squat raves, weirdos clubbing, reviews of new drugs, bits on club kids and their messy flats, before cutting out the weirdest pictures to adorn my walls with, a sort of to-do list of chaos.

Those important formative teenage years that shape you saw me face down in magazines that championed heroin chic as a movement, actively encouraging us to look like total shit, and I ate it up. Kind of fab in a Tom Ford for Gucci campaign, but famously it's not a *GREAT* lifestyle choice outside of that. All these avenues compounded and gave me the idea that fucking yourself up is a great idea. I buried my emo teenage feelings of self-loathing deep down inside and dealt with it by getting black-out drunk; after all, everyone else was doing it down in That London and they were having a whale of a time! What could go wrong?! Well . . .

Quite a lot actually.

The sense of partying was in the air. It wasn't just me. Geography has something to do with it. Manchester is a thirsty city, ingrained with an ethos of going out. Out all night and then into the next day, and then out-out again. And in the 90s Manchester was still riding the wave of the Hacienda, a club famed for its grimy hedonism. And with family friends talking about it like it was a pilgrimage to Lourdes, staying out all night became my heartfelt desire. While other kids dreamt of meeting Take That, I dreamt of raving till dawn and coming home with a cough. (Happy to say I made that particular dream come true quite a lot.)

As well as geography, science had something to do with it too: it's genetic y'see, I come from good raving stock. Our Irish roots provided the wanton need to chat to everyone and any-one, plus an unquenchable thirst for the good stuff made me quite the pro at drinking. And we're quite a thirsty family, a skill we inherited from our mother. I'm not saying she's a bad influence, but she's Courtney Love for those in their late seventies. Now just to clarify, she's not a pisshead, nor has she ever had a problem with alcohol (apart from when the shop's shut – wheeeyyyyyy!). But she does have a problem with going to bed early; she LOVES a party. She is not a lush, but she can put away her fair share of G&Ts without any consequences apart from a mildly red face. She's fun, never messy, and I've never seen her 'drunk' (like her kids have been) in my life. At most she may find a not-so-funny pun-based joke absolutely hilarious. Now, I didn't inherit this aspect of drinking, the joyfulness of drink being an optional side dish to a night out. No, on my night outs booze was the starter, main course and dessert. Putting alcohol in Eileen merely makes her more up for a conversation, more up for staying up setting the world to rights. Putting alcohol in me is similar to when you pour it on a Christmas pudding and light it – BOOM! THAR SHE BLOWS! An out-of-control booze-fuelled fire decimating the pudding. I'm the pudding, charred and carbonised.

I didn't really notice Eileen's knack for the fear-free boozin' till after my dad died back in 2016.

We entered a new relationship when he passed and once our grieving had settled. A very social and restorative and, well, a fun relationship. We became a little boozy duo, a fun-time girlie and her GBF on the daytime cocktails. Quite *SATC*. We took holidays together, went to Fashion Week, had Valentine's Day getting pissed at Nobu cos we were both single. We were living like Bonnie and Clyde on the run from being alone. I'd make her come to London to stay up late, take her to house parties and fly to New York on a whim to see *Saturday Night Live*, where we'd stay up all night at the afterparty till dawn.

'That's where you get it from,' Our Jane says, and she's right. If the booze is flowing and the good times are rolling then so are we. What did I say? It's genetic. I can't help it! I'm just not as good as her on the sauce.

I wanted to make sure Eileen wasn't feeling alone when Dad died. So in the summer of 2018 when I left the Radio 1 Breakfast show and wanted to celebrate, I invited Eileen to join me and my mates in Mallorca. After the initial 'Ooooh I don't know' about whether or not she could face it, she came and day-drank us under the table. Our initial welcome lunch was at 2 p.m. and we ended up getting in at 4 a.m. In my excitement at not having to get up at 5 a.m. any more, we raged through a beach lunch boshing back bottles of rosé and then on to a bar in our wet swimming trunks for tequilas before singing through the tiny, mountain town back to our house. The next day was possibly *the* worst hangover of my life. I was bed-bound, crying out for Rennies and dabbing my forehead with a cold flannel, thinking the end was nigh. Meanwhile, Eileen was right as rain.

'It's me three kidneys,' she said. 'I feel fine!'

How could I forget my mother has three kidneys? Really. It's medically confirmed. I don't know if she was born with them or if she's evolved while living. Her own body exhausted from its two measly kidneys trying to process the Sauvignon Blanc decided it was easier to grow another fucker to help. She could be in the Marvel Comic Universe with that mutation. Specialist skill: drinking a minibar dry. 'Take that, Thanos!'

I think she must have stolen one of mine in childbirth because now my hangovers are absolutely biblical. They're not like normal people's hangovers where they go to the gym or for a jog to 'shake it off'. I can't even walk to the toilet and I feel lucky if I survive the day. When I'm hanging I must lie very still for the following twelve to fourteen hours in complete silence with absolutely no light to dare come near my eyes. There's no water to pass my lips nor a tiny morsel of food, for fear of either, or both, coming straight back up again. A hangover in my house is the most dramatic of days, crying out in pain, sometimes raising the energy to sip a Lucozade and dry-choke down a chip or two from McDonald's around 5 p.m. They used to be quite funny when I was in my twenties and I'd head off to record a TV show after no sleep whatsoever, or go to a fashion show and sit front row, smuggling in a Corona to take the edge off, but now I genuinely want to call the hospital.

But it wasn't JUST the drink that got our family going; we just LOVED a party, I did, even as a six-year-old. Not just a kids' party; I loved a dinner party with the adults too. After complaints of feeling out of place, the one situation where I really came into my own was at parties. Not the fellow kids parties down Wacky Warehouse but family parties with my mum's entourage of middle-aged cronies. Any cause for celebration meant a buffet and everyone would come round. Now, what with my mum and dad not having me till they were in their forties, and me not being the biggest hit with pals my own age, my formative party years were forced to happen around a bunch of people in their mid-fifties. While normal twelve-year-olds were drinking White Lightning and smoking weed in the park, I was helping Mum prepare a prawn cocktail and a trifle for her friends who were coming round for 'Girls' Night'. 'Girls' Night' was and still is a deeply iconic evening that happens on the reg.

Each of the nine 'girls', a mixture of sisters and pals, would take turns in hosting a dinner party at their respective homes, and I got full-on party panic when it was Eileen's turn. They were an all-female force of Elnett set do's and angular bobs, dangly bejewelled clip-on earrings and sharp shoulder pads. I was obsessed. I'd beg to stay up late and force myself in between Auntie Sheila and Auntie Angela to ogle their fab outfits up close, smelling their floral perfumes and enjoying their hearty laughs.

But big family parties were my Superbowl; this time the partners would be allowed, so Girls' Night evolved into a multi-gendered mega-bash. I loved the mess and noise created by forty 'aunties and uncles', some real, some just my mum's mates, all shouting over one another and filling the house with stomping shoes on the wooden floors and clinking glasses. I'd squeeze through the crowd at (replacement) hip height to the adults, the smell of spilt Stella on the floor, and jump around from guest to guest saying hellos and collecting kisses from the aunties. I'd love the pre-party anticipation of Mum looking for the right glasses in the cupboard, all red in the face from the volcanic heat of the pans bubbling and boiling away:

'Pete, I can't find the bloody key for the window, it's like a furnace in here.'

Dad would swear under his breath while looking for this minuscule key to open the window before a last-minute dash to the Co-op cos 'there's no bleedin' beers in, Eileen!'

Even the thrill of people wearing shoes inside the house got me going; seeing Mum in a two-inch wedge heel sent me over the edge. 'SHE'S BASICALLY BIANCA JAGGER AT STUDIO 54!' There'd be flans and quiches, jelly and trifles – and my personal highlight: a clear sign that this wasn't a regular night, it was a party night:

Crisps

in

a

bowl.

Nothing said sense of occasion to me more than some decanted salt and vinegar Walkers plonked in a salad bowl. So extravagant! So generous! And when Eileen set down a four-way dip box selection, well, we were living like royalty.

Eileen dressed for occasions like this, out came the outfits – a pillar-box red suit jacket with matching knee-length pencil skirt, and she'd clip on gold bulky earrings and throw on a chunky necklace, brushing her fringe with her fingers and a 'do I look all right?' as she rushed down the stairs, straightening up her skirt, to welcome the guests. I'd race to the front door, squeezing in front of Eileen as she opened it to a merry band of middle-aged cronies carrying an assortment of home-made riches all encased in foil. A trifle from one, some coleslaw from another and, my personal favourite, Auntie Carmel's cheese and onion pie. The pie was the stuff of legend, prompting an orchestral 'oooooooooh' from the guests when the foil was pulled back and the pie was revealed. There was often a round of applause.

'Oh it's just cheese and onion,' a bashful Auntie Carmel would say to quiet the pie-starved rabble.

I'd be tasked with taking everyone's coats. I'd take them upstairs, launching them onto my bed without a care, scared to miss any of the action downstairs. I'd be the only child at these gatherings; the offspring of the other couples were actual adults with jobs and their parents were experiencing a new chapter of life after children. Finally time to enjoy adult company again, an evening of fine conversation, wine and— 'Hiyyaaa!' cue me coming downstairs with my trumpet. After annoying them all with my inane chatter, I would feel that it was time for a musical interlude. Forcing my way through the oldies, I'd stand in the centre of the room and wait.

'ARE YOU ALL LISTENING?' I'd ask, before demanding that they had to pay attention but not look directly at me while I performed. A request later copied by many a female diva.

After a few minutes of erratic tootlings I'd await the applause, bow and thank them for their time, before leaving the stage and suggesting some music to keep the vibe going: 'Shall we have a disco?'

I'd press play on Candi Staton on the CD player and my dad would start clapping, shrugging his shoulders up and down out of time while getting the lyrics wrong, as Auntie Carmel would grab my hands and say, 'Let's have a jive! Yer mum used to be the best jiver in town.'

We'd all dance around in a little circle in the lounge and I'd throw myself in the middle to breakdance and attempt a cart-wheel or two, before being told, 'Enough now, you're gonna be sick after all that pie.'

I'd stop and eventually go up to bed full of pie and, covered in carpet burns from my erratic performance, I'd fall asleep to the sound of adults chatting and clattering glasses and plates as they cleaned up the kitchen. Still to this day my optimum drifting-off-to-sleep soundtrack would be: ME IN BED AND SOMEONE IS TALKING AND CLEANING UP AFTER A PARTY.

Even coming downstairs the next day to see rows and rows of cleaned glasses made me feel content – and it still does now. The house would feel different, the energy refreshed, the walls all high on endorphins from human interaction. We'd have a fry-up as Eileen pretended not to be hungover: 'Ooooh it must have been something I ate, I think I overate. I wonder if it was that pie. Sometimes onion doesn't agree with me.'

These were my formative social moments; they made me love people, love parties and love a spectacle. Even if it was just some crisps in a bowl, I was hooked.

I wasn't into sport, I wasn't academic, I didn't love school, I didn't love anything really, apart from a party.

Seeing my mum and dad truly laugh was and still is my favourite thing. And they'd howl laughing. I saw them as different people at parties; they weren't JUST these vessels of instruction. They weren't there to parent, to dictate or rule or complain or do boring parent things. They had this other life, of being, well, fun. I started to think, how could I make that feeling last forever? How could I have fun all the time?

Obviously I couldn't hit the sesh at this age, so it was quite the wait until I was privy to the experience of an adult all-dayer. It was Christmas Day, I was aged fourteen, and while Eileen peeled sprouts I headed to the local pub in Chadderton with Our Andrew and his mates. All the lads in their new Christmas Stone Island and me in a new pale green merino wool Armani jumper that I had begged for. This is the life, I thought. Here I was, in the pub with Our Andrew's mates in football hooligan-approved branded clothing, necking the pints, on my way to being the SESH KING I dreamt of becoming.

I watched Andrew like a cub learning from the adult lion. He was a generous ringleader, getting the beers in for all the lads and cracking gags, and as I laughed along I matched them pint for pint. First one, no problem, went down like a dream. Refreshing, crisp, cold and just what the doctor ordered. We carried on and after five whole pints of Stella, I'm not OK hun. I'm fucking wasted. I staggered back into the house trying to hold it together in front of Pete and Eileen and hit the deck of the hall. 'Just gonna have a lie-down,' I managed to say as

I dragged myself up and staggered up the stairs in my prized jumper.

'He's pissed out his head!' Pete said. 'What've you done to him? And don't be sick on that jumper!!' he screamed up the stairs.

'I won't, I jwust fwelll a bit fwunnny,' I said, eyes rolling back in my head.

'He only had a pint,' Andrew said, 'lightweight.'

I'd definitely had at least five and I was definitely a teenager who'd never been out drinking before. The room was spinning. The jumper had to come off. Downstairs I could hear the constant hum of a mild row as Mum prepared Christmas dinner. I'd never felt like this before. I was hot. I was cold. I was in motion. I tried to open the window, frantically searching for the key and some air to remedy this out-of-body experience. I needed to get it out of me. So I came up with a cunning plan to puke undetected. The window was the perfect route. Forgetting we had a conservatory, I heaved out the window. Vomit spewed from me and a plod-plod-plodding onto the PVC roof below woke my elderly gran from her afternoon nap, who then confusingly looked over her shoulder to locate the noise. An iconic start to my drinking career.

After that I was off on one.

Once I was sixteen I was free to go out-out, and boy did I love going out-out. Me and my mates Jenny and Kerry were a dynamic trio fuelled by Stella and Stone Roses, strutting around the Northern Quarter together before blagging it into Sankeys, a club in an old soap factory. My gran used to work in the factory before it became a club, so I felt like every hour on the dancefloor was essentially family time. I loved that dancefloor: the stickiness, the sweat, the bass in your chest rattling your teeth; it was everything I'd longed for and more. It was the sole focus of life for a few years and every now and then our hearts would break as we'd be refused entry for one thing or another. Once for turning up with a shattered bottle of red wine – frustrated that I couldn't get the cork out, I smashed the neck off on a wall and drank it directly from the bottle: 'You want some? You might get a bit of glass in yer mouth but you can spit it out,' I said to a fellow raver in the queue.

So off I went on a big old lifestyle booze cruise; like a crazed Jane McDonald all aboard the HMS *Stella Artois* I sailed the seas of the north-west, with steady tides and sunny days, until one day I came over a little funny.

By the time I arrived at uni in Liverpool I had three years of the sesh under my belt. On one of my very first days, I was walking to the library and all of a sudden felt sick to my core, frozen in fear. A heavy overwhelming sense of confusion descended on me. I felt like I was on the edge of a cliff, it was crumbling beneath my feet.

I wanted to call my mum.

'Mum, I feel funny,' I said, voice all shaky.

'Like what, love?' she said

'I don't know. I can't explain it. It's like when you're in school and someone comes in and interrupts class and goes "Can Nick Grimshaw go to the headmaster's office please?",' I said.

'Ah, you probably have a little bit of anxiety,' she said. 'Have you been taking care of yourself?'

'No. Why, was I supposed to?'

10

That London

I always had a fascination with 'That London'. Never called just London; the added 'That' was a telling dislike of the city by the north. It was sniffed at by my friends and family as a whimsical, soft place full of fairies. So obviously I was sold.

Before making the move to live in our beloved capital, I'd only been twice. The first time I came home with a carrot fish.

I'd been down to St Albans to visit Eileen and Pete's old pals, the wonderfully named Hugh and Sylvia. It seemed like everyone down in London had musical names that sung off the tongue. Hugh and Sylvia served us salad in their garden and Our Jane was allowed to go to Camden Market, while I stayed with the olds. The next day we went for a Chinese, which was like going to the moon for me. Not a Chinese chippy takeaway – a real restaurant with Chinese food in it. I screamed at the chopsticks: MUM MUM MUM LOOK AT THESE! Flinging noodles and beansprouts across the room. In the centre of the table was something I couldn't get my head round: a bright orange statue of a goldfish shooting out of the water surrounded by splashes as it leapt out for air.

'It's made of carrot, they carve animals out of carrot here,' Sylvia told me.

My head blew up. What! What the hell happens down here in London! Up north we're having frozen crispy pancakes and down here there's carrot art on the table. I kept one eye on the carrot goldfish as I tried to work the chopsticks, before finally being given a fork. At the end of the meal I was allowed to take the fish home. They put it in an ice cream tub with water and I cared for it like it were a real fish. I don't think show and tell was a thing at my school, but back there the next day I sure decided it would be. It was now a little browned around the edges, but I showed off this fishy carrot as proudly as if I had carved it myself, carrying it above my head through the playground like one of the three wise men with mysterious frankincense to show the baby Jesus. The class 'ooooweddd' and 'ahhhhhed' at my carrot in an ice cream box as I told them of magical far-away London.

Oldham felt a million miles from London. Oldham is on the outskirts of Manchester. At school people called Oldham 'town' and Manchester 'Manchester', but in our house, ruled by die-hard proud Mancunians, Oldham was Oldham and 'town' was Manchester. I loved going into town with Eileen and Pete as a kid, I loved the thrill that came with feeling on edge here, the intimidation of the big city filled with shifty people who had a pace about them. We'd park at the cheap parking on the outskirts of the Northern Quarter or by Strangeways Prison and walk into the centre past the derelict warehouses looking like New York in a film.

We'd walk faster here and I'd search the floor with my eyes, getting jazzed up by all the smashed bottles, taking in the layers of fly-postered club nights now peeling off the wall. We'd see ladies working the street corners in the daytime and I'd think about where they were sleeping and where they lived. I'd be silently worrying about them all the way home.

Something about the chaos of the city called me. I liked the feeling there; bigger, stranger, rougher, dirtier. But even though I liked it I'd reach out to hold my mum or Our Jane's hand. I refused to do so in our safe town of Royton but I needed the family reassurance here.

There is a warm sense of pride in the city that I love. It feels like our hearts belong in Manchester. It was there that Eileen and Pete were born, where they met, where they danced the nights away in the 1960s. They were proper townies, living the best 1960s Manchester could offer, Pete from Collyhurst where he was born into prefabricated housing and Eileen, the posher of the two, growing up in Moss Side. It was Moss Side in the centre of Manchester where I was born in the hot summer of 1984, a few years after the infamous riots that were dubbed an 'orgy of violence' by our local paper.

On the way home from town we'd go and see Gran Beattie. She was mega, as solid and northern as they come. She was born in actual ye olden times – in 1912, a date that used to shock my classmates as all their grans were about forty-five. Beattie was cute and cuddly but not your regular nan-pushover; she had the no-nonsense hardness about her that came with living through two world wars. She was matter-of-fact, sharp as a knife, busy and funny way up into her mid nineties. I loved Gran Beattie and she loved me. She actually loved me the most out of all the five grandkids – I know this because she told me. And even more brutally: them. She tripled up on my school photos, in comparison to their one or maybe even none. What can I say? She was a woman of taste. Gran Beattie lived in Moston, a stone's throw away from the city centre and more recently made famous by the rapper Aitch. Like Aitch she was dead Manc, very proud to be Manc, with the Manchesterness oozing out of her. Unlike Aitch, she didn't have mad bars. She was the most northern a nan could be and, conversely, the least London a person could be. There was an unwritten rule growing up in the 0161 area that London was for wankers. So breaking the news that I was to move down carried a Shakespearean level of guilt. It was not only betraying your family and friends, but a betrayal of the north.

'London??! Oh. You're not going all the way to London for work!?' Gran Beattie took the news I was heading down south like a bullet to the chest, one hand raised to her head in disbelief.

'Are you sure?' she went on. 'The pavements are very 'ard down there. Very, very 'ard.'

'What?' we all asked.

'The pavements! Very 'ard! On yer feet!!' she shouted back, 'I went down for the day once and our shoes, ooooooh, well, they were worn out from the pavements. Worn them right out!' She slapped her hands together, imitating the sound of her beating feet against the concrete, shaking her head in disgust.

All us Grimmys fell silent and looked confused as we tried to figure out what she meant. We had no clue. I've lived in London for nearly sixteen years now, and I still have no idea what she was on about.

Before we had time to ask her to explain she was off again.

'Where will you get yer hair cut?' she asked, 'Will they have somewhere?'

The family were now falling about sweetly laughing at the thought of millions of poshy Londoners managing to live life without any hairdressers and very worn-out holey shoes.

'Of course they have hairdressers, Gran!' I exclaimed. And they did, my first of which was £6 at Mr Toppers on Camden High Street and it was an absolutely absurd indie haircut. Think Gareth from *The Office*. Maybe Beattie had a point.

'What will you eat?' Her next frantic question and a question constantly asked by grans and nanas the world over, none more so than up north.

'They don't have gravy down there y'know! On their chips. No proper gravy.'

And those were Gran Beattie's concerns. Shoes, hair, gravy. In that order. I should've called this book *Shoes, Hair, Gravy*.

Gravy was, and still is, a big concern among my northern mates, 'They don't have owt wet on their tea in That London,' said my friend Jenny, 'Weirdos.'

Guilt and gravy: the two biggest concerns at this time in my life. Guilt at betraying Manchester for London; and my relationship with gravy was over, a lifetime of gravy-free, dry chippy teas ahead of me.

Once I moved down south I had no idea what Gran Beattie was on about with the worn-out shoes and no-hairdressers arguments, but the gravy one rang true. It may only be two hours away on the train but it was a world away in terms of culinary delights. If the north were gravy, London would be rosemary-doused flatbread and hummus.

Not long after I'd moved to London I went back one weekend. I offered to do my mum's shopping list at the Big Tesco, and thought I'd mix it up with a few London discoveries. I popped in some hummus, sweet potatoes and soya milk. The reaction was like I'd started smoking crack.

'What THE BLEEEEDIN HELL IS ALL THIS?' Pete screamed. 'Eileen, get a load of this . . .' Lifting up items in genuine disgust, shock and awe. 'What the bleedin 'ell is "Ummmmmusssss"?'

I began to explain: 'It's a chickpea purée, famous all ove—'

'What the bleeding hell is a chickpea?!' Pete getting more irate. 'We just wanted some bleedin' bread!'

I knocked them up a meal I'd learnt from the Londoners – roasted sweet potato, hummus on the side for dipping and some lentil salad.

'Jesus Christ,' Pete said, 'the bleedin' ell is all this . . .'

Eileen shot him a look to shut up and wiggled her fingers over the plate, not knowing where to begin.

'Ooooh it looks delicious this, I bet it's good on my WeightWatchers plan this,' she said.

'Are these carrots cooked?' Pete said, looking like he was eating actual cat shit.

'It's a sweet potato, Dad.'

He shook his head, muttering 'SWEET potato' to himself over in a Peter Kay Garlic Bread stylee. Peter Kay's 'Garlic bread' stand-up routine was less of a comedy act for northern families and more a realistic piece of documentary footage. He carried on chewing it down, huffing and puffing like a kid who's been forced to eat their greens.

From then on I was the bane of their existence when it came to eating, claiming that he 'only eats London food!'

'He's mad! He's lost it!' Pete would shout in the background on the phone when Eileen would call to check in what I'd be having for dinner. It was simple, I just wanted non-dairy milk.

'NON-DAIRY! BLOODY 'ELL! NOWT WRONG WI' COWS,' Pete would shout in the background. 'Coming up here with his London ways!'

They thought I was hysterical, Eileen throwing her hands up to her temples in disbelief as if I'd been lost to showbiz in London town, all cos I wanted to just eat the odd salad and avoid milk from a cow.

I wasn't too picky, just the London-ness of trying to not eat that much gluten and avoid dairy had seeped in. One summer I dabbled in veganism, and tried to explain the benefits of it to Pete, which went down like when someone tried explaining NFTs to me. Thankfully that only lasted three days and then I broke my spell as a vegan by accidentally eating a Scotch egg, the least vegan snack on the planet.

Years later when I had to prank them on my radio show I listed an array of outrageous shopping items. I knew it was an easy one to get them going. I requested wheatgrass, caviar and an ostrich egg, as I needed a large egg for this new diet I was on. I played it out on air to millions and still to this day get daily DMs about Eileen and Pete's severe reaction, each item causing their brains to blow up a little more.

'WHEATGRASS?'

'CAVIAR??'

'OSTRICH EGG?... Can't you just have two normal eggs?!'

I should explain how I got to be this London wanker who DARED AVOID COW'S MILK and how I got to London in the first place. I knew I wanted to be on the radio but Radio 1 wasn't just gonna come knocking on my front door in Oldham; I thought it more likely they'd have me if I went to them. By some miracle I got an interview at MTV, so That London it was.

'What are you gonna wear for it?' Our Jane said, asking all the important questions.

'What the bleedin 'ell is MTV?' asked my dad with a straight face.

'The United channel?' he continued with a glimmer of hope in his eyes – maybe I'd turned my back on homosexuality and my love for frivolous pop culture.

'No, it's a music channel,' I explained.

'A music channel? Oh bleedin' 'ell, that's not a proper job,' he complained as he flicked his newspaper back open.

'What job is it?' Eileen asked, with promise.

'And what's the pay?!' Pete increasingly excited at the prospect of me fucking off out his house.

The thing was, I didn't know the answer to any of these questions apart from what MTV was, and after growing up in a Sky-free household with a measly four channels, I was even vague about that. In my haste to get to London and out of Oldham (no offence), and some wise words from Our Jane, 'WHATEVER YOU DO, DON'T BE AN ACCOUNTANT' (Our Jane is an accountant), I was determined to find a job that was fun, so I applied to literally EVERYTHING available in the media, qualified or not. In true bimbo style, I looked at the jobs available and applied to the ones that seemed to have a nice place for lunch nearby. 'Oooh that one's near Fabric,' I thought as I set about building my future around easy access to a night out. A runner at ITV, a sound trainee at Channel 4, a marketing intern for the BBC and even a broadcast assistant at good old Radio 1, who turned me down. Twice. I even have the letter to prove it, handily framed in a chic mahogany picture frame by my mother as a very random passive-aggressive Christmas gift one year.

In my mind at that time MTV just felt like where I should be, faffing around in London and watching Missy Elliott videos. They had about eight different internships available on their website. Suitable for none, I decided to apply for all eight. And interest came back from their international creative department. Hoorah! I was up for an interview to be the intern in the international creative department! Great! Wait, what the HELL is that?!

Rather than figure it out, I prioritised and went back to Our Jane's pressing question – WHAT WAS I GOING TO WEAR? I mean, what do you wear to your first proper adult job interview at MTV, whose office happened to be in London's indie capital, Camden?

Me and Our Jane headed to Urban Outfitters, which back in 2006 seemed decidedly fashion-forward and 'very London', we thought. I had no money, so Jane offered to foot the bill. I opted for the jean fit of the time – black spray-on skinny ones – a white shirt, black skinny tie and a black V-neck jumper; think Franz Ferdinand's first day at school. Off I went on the train to London town, where, like any professional starting their media career, I headed to the Lock Tavern (which I'd read about in the *NME*) for a pre-interview pint. The audacity of turning up for an interview, with no prep, no idea what the department does, and choosing to get a pint over doing any sort of research, actually makes me feel hot with cringe.

It must have been a magical pint because I got the job. A few weeks later, and after months of rejection letters from across the media landscape, MTV were the ones to fall for my bullshit— I mean, appreciate my CV.

So I had a job; now I just needed a place to stay. So I did the most peak 2006 thing possible: struck a deal over MySpace with Queens Of Noize. And yes that is a Z instead of an S. It was indie sleaze! They didn't have time for a regular S! Who did?! The Queens of Noize were Mairead and Tabitha, a dynamic duo of loveable indie DJing babes who bumbled their way around London with the Libertines, Kate Moss and

Courtney Love in tow. Their chaotic lives spilled out in the pages of my bible of the time, the *NME*, where they went on all-dayers with Lisa Moorish and Graham Coxon. They were the scene queens, becoming a pair of Edie Sedgwicks for a more smelly generation. I'd met them when I interviewed them for my university radio show; I went and sat on the floor of their dressing room and quizzed them on life on the *NME* tour. We instantly bonded and, ever the professionals, decided to go on a 24-hour bender all around Liverpool. It was a night where they gave me a DIY haircut and I forked out all my student loan on repairing a giant window I accidentally smashed in an unfortunate attempt at a party trick involving a heavy ashtray.

I slid into Mairead's DMs and broke the good news about my job.

Eileen and Pete thought they were silly. I thought they were everything, key to my first major life decision. Moving to London then for me was like moving to live on Pluto or summat, full of impossibility and out of my reach. The indie nonchalance for which they were known also turned out to double up as great career advice: 'Nah fuck it, come on, you can always move back.' Sound advice.

As well as being my career advisors they were also to be my new landlords. The MySpace deal I struck up was this: I could stay at Tabitha's flat for free while she was in Mexico for a few months, if I worked for free, flyering for their club, and doing the door on a Friday night. Being a loyal subject to the high court of indie back then, I was like, where's the catch? Deal!

Off I went to London with my army jackets and horrible pointy boots, to live in a flat I'd never seen that belonged to some random girl I'd met once.

I arrived knowing basically no one; I had a few raver mates from uni who were scattered around the city but it was a fresh start for me, one that I was really excited about. I loved everything about London when I arrived; I got straight on the Tube to Camden and rode it like it was a theme park rollercoaster, with a stupid grin across my face. I got out and tried not to look like a tourist, copying the ways of the angry Londoners, all of whom walked with such urgency it was as if they were on the way to douse a fire, running around the tunnels of the Underground at doctors-in-A&E speed. Not smiling, huffing and puffing at anyone daring to walk near them and avoiding eye contact with all other humans. My bags briefly got in the way of a nice-looking lady as I tossed and turned to check which way I needed to go for the Tube.

'Oh, ooops, oh, sorry,' as I did that annoying thing of getting more in her way.

'For fuck's sake,' she said, sharply and sternly, as she navigated her way around my northernness.

It was the hearty welcome I'd been after; I even loved that. Unclear if I was on ecstasy when I arrived, but I was looking at the London Underground with severe beer goggles on.

'Wow, it stinks down here!' I thought, 'I love it!' Skipping along smiling, almost high-fiving suicidal bank workers, and finding the mice running along the Tube tracks adorable like some demented underground Snow White.

I was a little more nervy than I'd have liked to be by the time I got off the Tube sheepishly in Camden. The reality of life on the backstreets of Camden Town was a little less attractive than I'd conjured up on the train ride down. I was like my mum on holiday, looking over my shoulder, paranoid everyone was out to mug me. Have I really just moved to a random person's flat in a city I don't know? To do a job I don't know anything about? And work for a club night I've actually never been to? It was a sharp gear-shift from the single bed at Eileen and Pete's with the suburban wood pigeons cooing away as my only soundtrack.

I dragged my bags up to Tabitha's flat, my new home, and figured out what to wear for day one at MTV. The air was thick with the sound of guitars and Razorlight's 'Golden Touch' was blasting from my MySpace homepage, so in true Johnny Borrell style I opted for head-to-toe white. White spray-on jeans, white T-shirt, white cardigan and dirty white Converse. Quite the look, I thought.

I walked down the hill to work, which was right in the middle of Camden – actually I almost ran there, full of excitement.

It turned out my job was nuts. I'd be tasked with searching through old MTV footage for shots of a particular pop star in a particular look we wanted to reference before building a mini stage for an advert we would be making from cardboard. Then I had to make my hand into a mini rock star for the mini stage by painting on a little leather jacket and hand-sized guitar. Gruelling stuff. This didn't feel like work.

There were all sorts of people at MTV. I was in the international department and you could tell: we had graphic designers who were Spanish, Norwegian, Korean, an Australian boss, Turkish colleagues, and I loved it. The only time I'd heard a European accent before was on holiday. There was all sort of accents. Except northern ones. I made friends with Gillian from marketing, who was from Oxfordshire – she said things like 'grraaaaasssss' and 'baaaaaaath', stretching out all her vowels all the way to the home counties. Her voice sang merrily out of her mouth. I basically thought anyone south of Birmingham was dead posh. I remember thinking should I start saying graaaassssss?

I tried to match their ways and starting drinking things I'd never heard of like a flat white. Maybe it was a delicious chip on my own shoulder but I felt like the odd one out again. I felt poor and thick.

One day walking to work I was approached with an 'oi!'

It wasn't the posh southern voices I'd heard before in the office. Whereas they were Mary Poppins, this was Dick Turpin.

I looked back and saw this tiny little beehived mentalist I'd seen round Camden before, dropping into a light jog to catch up with me. It was a pre-'Rehab'/'Back To Black' Amy Winehouse. I'd not met her before but loved her first album *Frank*, and had previously queued behind her in Pret as she quizzed a very confused Spanish man about whether or not the chilli con carne soup had carbs in it.

'Well, has it?' she asked. ' Is it chilli con carne-flavour soup or just like chilli con carne in a soup?' Getting increasingly more annoyed at their confusion, she carried on: 'Like is it chilli con carne-flavoured soup or is there rice in it or what?' She kissed her teeth and barged out, no soup.

This morning on my way to work, I waited as she caught up with me and hit me with questions: 'All right stalker? I always see you, what you doin'? What you doin' up this early? Where you from? You're northern innit? Ah I love a northerner,' she said to me, in her Reebok classics and Fred Perry shirt. She dropped me off at work like a very aggressive nanny and headed off on her merry way. Later that day after work I saw her in the pub and we decided to get drunk. She was my first introduction to London without pretension, a Londoner that even my northerners back at home would like. Not one of these airy fairy flat-white-drinking types. She was the real London in a person: hard, charming, brash, smart, sexy, semi-scary and intoxicating. She could have been any age, twelve or sixty-eight, with this sometimes childlike demeanour popping out from the *Carry On Cockney* character to say hello.

I remember thinking I wanted to be more like her – not the famous jazz singer with a beehive bit, but I wanted to have the bravado she carried herself with, waltzing through the pub with the swagger of a Polly Pocket-sized Liam Gallagher. She wasn't one of those that changed to suit the mood of others, something a people-pleaser like me is guilty of. Whereas my body language is often 'like me like me', hers was 'fuck off'. Her hardness fit my softness. And we bumbled our way around day-drinking and getting into rows with people for a summer or two. She had this great flat that became the place for after-hours and we'd all go back to hers and fire up her electric sunbed. We'd sit on the floor side by side and toss our heads back into it to tan our faces while smoking fags and drinking a mini Red Stripe.

In a world full of frivolous party chatter, her words had weight. She would instantly disarm you, sitting down like a burly bloke, with legs wide open, staring into your eyes and asking, 'How are you baby?', stroking your head with warm assurance, forcing you to open up like a therapist. By the time you could answer she'd be off: 'Cool baby cool, one sec.' And off she'd go behind the bar to serve bemused customers a pint on one of her charitable shifts at The Hawley Arms. The pub was packed with people my age all working these mental jobs I'd never heard of, or not working at all.

We were thrown together through parties where we partied all night, and before long the odds and sods from around London formed a little family. We were all away from home, all on some mission of self-discovery, and craved the cosiness of Sunday roasts from time to time, an elixir to the partying. Heading down south solo with no prior London pals meant that my bond with people accelerated. I'd meet someone and then that night sleep on their couch or move in with them for a brief time, or, my dad's fave: bring them home to Manchester for Christmas.

As soon as the clock struck 6 p.m. at MTV, we'd be out of there and it was every person for themselves as we speed-walked the short journey to the Hawley, taking in that first pint, gasping as if we'd been down the mines for fourteen hours.

'Tough day at the office?' Dougie, the barman, would say.

'Yeh man, I had to paint my hand green,' I'd reply before ordering another.

The pub would fill up with MTV folk and the faces of the high street regulars, the old man I'd chat to of a morning, the coffee seller from the market and the odd person off the telly. Before long it would be heaving and by 9 p.m. on most weeknights you'd have a party on your hands. It was the glory days of Camden, this little-known pub The Hawley Arms became a youth centre for alcoholic adults. Just like they do in *EastEnders* or *Corrie*, you could wander up to the pub solo and run into everyone you'd ever met, no pre-planning needed, you'd just roll up. I first went on a Friday in April 2006 and then proceeded to go every single night for about the next five years. That first Friday in the pub was like the start of something special, the first episode in a very long, very drunken, mega-series of nights outs. Every night out either began there, stayed there or ended up there. So much happened there. I fell down the stairs there, had lock-ins there, slept there, had birthdays there: on one of which I dressed as Jesus and made everyone come as religious icons; Eileen was furious.

London was absolutely mental to me. It was an endless carousel of parties and people. I was free to rage seven nights a week and our MTV credentials meant we got invited to the launch of any dubious new product that we'd happily go along to. A new disgusting flavour of cider? Sure, I'll be there! The new Diesel Shower Gel? I wouldn't miss it for the world!

Before long I was so comfortable at MTV that I fell back into the class clown routine I'd dabbled in at primary school. I'd call around on the work landline to confirm the RSVP for a party I'd been forwarded and add on my name and a few others. My boss would be waiting next to me for me to step off the call.

For a newbie in the capital it wasn't long before I got into the swing of it. I figured out where to go, where not to go; mainly where we'd get free drinks and where we'd have to pay. I was on the strictest budget and not in any position to be turning up my nose at a free drink. It was more opening your throat and chugging it down in one. Like an indie sleaze Oliver Twist, I was insatiable for the drink.

'Please sir, can I have some more?'

'More? MORE? Why yes of course you can – it's 2006 and you have no responsibilities!' Yay!

Nights out consisted of an incomprehensible amount of random parties that we were probably not invited to, and the same amount of free drinks. We'd bumble from party to party collecting fellow thirsty revellers. Before long a troupe of thirsty jobless wonders would amass, like a giant tumbleweed of liggers, and off we'd go till 4 a.m., raging around for no reason other than it was a Wednesday. I'd keep a toothbrush and change of clothes in my desk drawer, often coming in, live and direct, from an afterparty, brushing my teeth for the first time in twenty-four hours in the work bogs. We'd be out-out on the daily inviting myself to Fashion Week, squeezing onto the front row of a Gareth Pugh show with an oversized Tiger beer on the knee of a Geldof. Any Geldof. Just not Bob.

London became uni on a GIGANTIC scale and the entire city felt like our campus. I felt right at home. Maybe it was the gallons of booze but I was really in love with this new stage of my life. It was all fresh and exciting to me, falling in love with everything and everyone down in That London. I was in love with the bricks of the houses, the curved white terraced houses that lined the streets of Camden next to 60s council blocks. It smelt different, the air was different, the water was cloudy and tasted funny, the showers encrusted with a hardened sheen of the ancient pipes, but I loved it all.

It was the summer of 2006 and nu-rave was in the air and we spent our nights out staying up at all-night raves and heading to secret Klaxons afterparties. Whereas at school I'd felt in competition with other people, not as book-smart or able to concentrate in lectures, London got rid of that. Everyone was on different pages of their lives, everyone had wildly different jobs, everyone was exploring different stages of ups and downs, all different ages but together. There were people in their forties down the boozer raging till dawn with kids of eighteen (some of whom were their actual kids), ex-rock stars partied with new artists and there was a freedom in the air that I'd never felt before. And have definitely not since. We were the last social media-free party generation. We were free to not look perfect and even more free to look like total shit.

After nine months of being an absolutely shit intern, my contract was up and suddenly I was on the dole; the pub was now my sole priority. It was around this time that stuff started to change. I don't know what was in the water but everyone seemed to have a dream. And then one by one they just made them come true. It seemed like everyone around me got their break: Amy became famous, Aggy became a supermodel, Henry became a celebrated designer, Caroline Flack and I started doing TV with Alexa. It felt limitless and abundant, a time for yeses and can-dos.

Was it the freedom to be expressive? Was it that we didn't spend all our time on our phones? We didn't encourage each other, we certainly didn't talk about careers or goals out loud, but all of sudden people were starting to be interested in what was going on in that pub and what we were up to. Those days in the pub were so good as it wasn't an exclusive club of a famous few; this was an enormous raving troupe of football hooligans, the ones on the telly their mere mascots.

Not to sound like yer nan but we didn't have Instagram back in my day, so the only viable way for us to remember what we'd done the previous evening was to pick up the *London Lite* or the *London Paper*, two free rags given out on street corners to chronicle what had happened the night before. They also contained actual world news and current affairs, but I'd skip through that to take a look at the IMPORTANT stuff in the party pages. Where I'd see Alice Dellal falling out of Bungalow 8 or Kelly Osbourne blurry-eyed falling out of Punk in Soho. You don't really see pictures like that any more. People falling on the floor with their lipstick smudged, cross-eyed with wet hair, staggering into the back of an Addy-Lee. A real moment in time. No filters.

No retouching. It was as real as it got. We got fucked up and that was that.

When little Liv, my niece, came down to visit aged twelve, she summed up why I felt like this in London; she put it perfectly as she stared out the window of a cab: 'No one looks the same.'

NO ONE

LOOKS

THE

SAME.

That was it. I didn't feel like a little outsider anymore cos there were no insiders.

'You mean everyone dresses like total shit.' Our Jane putting it another way.

In between nights of downing pints, chain-smoking and absolutely no sleep, every weekend we'd descend on our friend Sadie's house. Sadie was rich and had this house that was a sanctuary and provided us all with our introduction to self-care. It was a palace, Camden's nirvana; plant-lined giant steps led you up from the grubby north London streets like heaven's escalator into a serene Sunday pleasureland of peace. The hall bigger than my flat had banquette seating, giant orchids and multiple candles scenting the air as tiny little cloud dogs like cherubs yapped you in with a welcome. There'd be a roaring fire flickering as tuberose burned, scenting the room and weaving its floral decadence into the sumptuous velvet couch on which multiple waifs and strays were nestled, all here for the same thing. Protection. It was a sanctuary for us all. There'd be Mairead and Tabitha both nursing hangovers on one couch and the ever-hilarious Collette, the Manc jazz singer, in her sunglasses and beanie slumped on a beanbag. Around them, various other musicians, DJs, artists, models, basically anyone remotely homeless, displaced and without a proper job raided Sadie's fridge and watched her telly.

'Alcohol is TERR-I-BLE for you,' Collette said in her thick northern accent, her voice battered from smoking and screaming, 'it is poison you know, actual poison, I've been POISONED! ohmygod do you think I've been actually poisoned? Ohhh bloody 'ell . . .'

Mairead and I would giggle as she repeated it over and over, pacing the floors while smoking (still with her sunglasses on), a sight we'd see at least twice a week, spinning the narrative that WE made her drink and SHE didn't actually like it.

'Have some charcoal and milk thistle,' Sadie suggested.

WHAT? WAIT? What are you actually on about? Charcoal? In your mouth? Back home the hangover cure was a lot more primitive: beg your mum to drive you to McDonald's and then have a pint again around 4 p.m.

Like I said, London was wild. And I loved it. Before long Sadie invited me into her family where I slept soundly and safely, waking up to a big family breakfast and days camped out with the kids. They were a second family to me and Eileen worried she was going to get some sort of bill at the end.

With MTV being over I needed to get on with my dream, the entire reason I was in London at all: Radio 1. I knew where the offices were because my dad had brought me as a kid.

*　　*　　*

Presumably someone had dropped out because one year when I was about thirteen Pete invited me to watch United away at Charlton Athletic. I excitedly signed up for it and found the map of London my dad had kept from about 1968 and placed it out on the living room floor, crawling over it to get a closer look at where we were staying.

'The hotel we're staying at is right by Radio 1!' I said.

'Oh,' he replied with zero excitement.

A man of his age thought Chris Evans and Sara Cox were 'bleedin' idiots' playing 'bloody garbage' and they needed to 'get something decent on' like 'the Beatles'.

'Fantastic city is London . . . If you got the money,' he said to me on the way down. 'You need to get your head down in school if you wanna live here.'

By now I did want to live here, but I did not want to get my head down at school. I wanted to come here and do radio. I was like Billy Elliot, minus the talent, desperate to flee my northern roots and dance, I mean drink my way across the capital city.

When we arrived he took me to Langan's Brasserie, where he recited the names of some probably now-dead actors who used to go here in the 60s. Here I drank red wine for the first time, and knocked it back like it was Ribena. It wasn't Ribena and I puked it up all over the walls of the Holiday Inn by Radio 1 in which we stayed. A memory etched into my head every day that I passed it for fourteen years of broadcasting at the BBC in later life.

Back then I was desperate to see Radio 1. So on the day before the match he took me down there and I tippy-toed through the windows peering into an empty Saturday-afternoon office. 'Woooow,' I said as I pressed my face up against the filthy London window and for a brief moment looked directly into my future. I wanted to say, 'It's mingin' in there, it looks like someone ransacked the staffroom at school,' but, weary of not wanting to have wasted my dad's time or put a damper on my dreams, I said, 'It's amazing.'

I looked back at my dad, a man who wanted nothing but the best for all of us, and said, 'I'm going to work here.'

I don't remember what he said or if he even said anything at all, but I remember the feeling. It was a feeling of realisation, of intent, of honesty. It felt momentarily like time stopped. Time to take in his smile and for him to take in my words.

Pete had his hands in his chino pockets and he cracked his warm smile that wrapped around his massive head, cheekily shrugging his shoulders with approval.

He repeated that moment to me before he died.

He told me the story sweetly and lovingly and recited my words to him; he reminded me of how I looked that day, what he saw and what I promised us both. He recited my words, impersonating little me. 'I'm going to work there, yer said to me,' before rounding it off with an '. . . and you did it.'

His full stop feeling more final than any full stop ever. 'You did it.'

It was the validation I didn't know I'd been searching for. It completed me somehow.

Me Dad's mate Gaga.

Me and Pixie in awe
of Fran in heels at
Glastonbury. Legend.

Every night was Friday
night back then. Now
every night is very much
Sunday night.

The attention on my first day of Breakfast could have made me an arsehole...

...but thankfully One Direction left me this very sweet note to keep me grounded. Thanks lads.

My friend Fifi said, 'Look terrible in your first BBC pass and then you will always look better when you leave.' Sound advice.

The chat that launched a thousand more... My very first TV interviewee ever: Kate Nash.

And my all time fave, the one and only Miss Robyn Rihanna Fenty.

Where I feel most at home: with a microphone, music and the attention of every single person ever.

One of the most famous, deeply iconic, chic, hilarious and gorgeous women in the world. And Kate Moss.

Mother at my 30th birthday party. A visual representation of where I get it from.

Me and Mama on our travels in Miami.

Me and Pete, who
I miss desperately.

Always sharp and
always considered,
I pray to be more Pete.

As a child I would annoy him
with shows in the living room.
And as an adult, I did the
exact same thing.

London meant friends became family. And their families became family too. Here we are on a family holiday in Ibiza.

Too close for comfort. Why watch TV in the lounge when you can watch it in bed?

Now I'm grown I've swapped the Spar for the spa.

Drake being very courteous after I puked in his flower pots.

Taking a load off in
Ibiza with Aimee.

Seen here with two legends
of the rave, Pete Tong and
Producer Fiona. Live and direct
from Amnesia straight to the
Radio 1 Breakfast Show.

Auditioning for The
Real Housewives Of
Beverley Hills.

Optimum softness. With the love of my life, my julie.

Still my most favourite memory of this city that adopted me. As I drove back to London after he died in Manchester, I knew there was a part of him that created my dream here, that would always stay with me here in 'That London'.

11

Pies Over Pop Stars

My mum and dad are lol. Or should I say my mum is lol and my dad was lol. He died back in 2016 just before Christmas and we felt the loss enormously. I'd never thought of my mum or dad dying, ever. Even when he had cancer I just didn't entertain him actually dying. Not Pete, he's too hard to die. So when he did, it naturally knocked me and the rest of the family sideways. He entered death in the same way he took on life, with pride and stoic confidence. He told me that I shouldn't be sad about death or him dying as 'it happens to everyone, no matter who you are.' He saw it as the great leveller and his outlook on death was like his one on life – you decide how you deal with it. He taught me many life lessons: a fool and his money are soon parted; if you work hard you make your own choices and if you don't someone else will make them for you. And there was the less inspirational and final line of 'You're gonna die one day too, son.' Not a life lesson maybe, just a hard cold fact that I nodded along to.

We loved him of course, like a family is obliged to, but we also ACTUALLY REALLY loved him, obsessed with all his ways, isms and lols. He was easily impersonated and our impressions

of him span generations, with his hot takes on sport and pop culture living on within our family like iconic ye-olden, hilarious
scripture. He did all the right dad stuff – provided for us, cared
for us; he inspired us, he encouraged us, supported us, we loved
him for thousands of reasons. But the top one of those thousands of reasons was the most important – he made us fucking
LAUGH. Intentionally or, more often than not, unintention-
ally, Pete was the source of some of the biggest pissing-your-
self-laughing-parts of my life.

Now if you'd heard my radio show you would have heard
Pete, either on air himself being pranked by me, or maybe I'd
slipped into my Pete schtick for a tale from our last family dinner. I loved to take on his voice and slide into what I thought
the Pete character was. Seemingly your average Manc man,
but actually on closer inspection, he was quite the avant-garde,
complex character. He was born on the breadline to a single
mother, unheard of in the 40s, which meant he grew up fast.
They lived in prefab housing, which is basically a Portakabin,
'like backstage at a festival?' I asked once to an eye-rolled
silence. When I'd be complaining about the hotel pancake
selection on holiday, or tapping my foot and sighing at the
buffet queue, he'd quickly remind me of the war and how he'd
survived on lard butties for most of his life.

He'd tell us stories of making DIY shoe insoles from scraps of
cardboard he found in the street and wedging them inside his
pumps to make the trip to school a little more comfortable. And
how he'd save up for bus fares so he could go for a dance at the
Plaza in town.

By fourteen he had finished school, was working and he was the man of the house. It was a big responsibility for little Pete, and I'm sure the sight of me at fifteen was a tough one for his eyes to focus on. He was bringing home a wage whereas I was huffing and puffing round the house because he wouldn't get me tickets to Destiny's Child.

He had to work hard and did so consistently for decades. As he grew up, so did his paycheque, and through that he discovered the finer things in life. He worked with iconic 80s and 90s brands like Perrier, Lean Cuisine and Nescafé. It all felt quite chic, quite Max and Susannah from *Brookside*. Pete got a company car and a mobile phone, the height of yuppie luxury as far as we were concerned. The lard butties were gone. As work started to foot the bill, he started to do boujie things like travel to Switzerland for a meeting, New York for a conference and Lake Como for a product launch. He got to eat at the finest restaurants in the world and sample first-class travel, no doubt made that little bit sweeter knowing that his hard graft had paid off and that these trips were being paid for by work. Gone were the cardboard insoles and in came leather brogues and sharp suits. He had gone from being the kid in temporary war housing to dining alongside movie stars in the greatest cities in the world. Essentially, he'd *changed*.

Apart from that . . . he hadn't really. And this is why I loved Pete: all of that and he also loved nothing more than fried egg and chips.

I only realised now that I saw his life as aspirational, not just the fab work trips but the love for the things that had made him, for the northern treats that signified home. I loved the way he could have both of these taste sensations intertwined, that he could love posh tea at the Waldorf Astoria but preferred the chippy in Rochdale. This was the food version of a mad person's iPod: Björk and Fatman Scoop. They all do their specific job, so why not enjoy scoffin' em all down at once? As a result of his varied culinary tastes he came to the conclusion that there were two kinds of food: good and bad. This outlook spread into other areas of his life, an arguably more important one: people. He either liked you or he didn't. I didn't realise how rare that was until I moved to London.

I loved when Pete arrived on the London scene, as he stepped off the Virgin Pendolino at 'Houston', as he inexplicably called it. His arrival was refreshing. His love of routine was almost like an art installation. Same outfits, same food, same likes. I used to think it was boring but now that I'm older I see it is DEEPLY chic. Imagine being so sure of how good you look that you wear the same outfit every day (clean, obviously). He had zero fucks to give. A symptom of working yourself out of a hellhole is: no one can tell you shit.

Back in 2006 when I started to be sucked into the world of celebrity nonsense via my job in London, it was obviously instantly hilarious to see those two worlds meet, the worlds of Pete and the paps. People can tend to get hysterical around a famous person. Not my dad. He had multiple run-ins with famouses, including some I'd bring home for sleepovers, but even if it had been the Dalai Lama at his doorstep, he still wouldn't give a shit. His nonchalance towards friends, celebrity or not, was the anchor I needed in not getting swept out to be lost at sea when I set sail for London. He read people instantly. Don't like them. Do like them. Famous or not, that's that.

Now, doing the telly and radio means you're given a sneak peek behind the curtain of celebrity. You can find yourself in random rooms waiting for Mary J. Blige or sharing a car with 50 Cent in New York and for a while, understandably, it feels absolutely insane. But over time you realise that these are just people too and they're people at work. They want to get this done and then leave and go home to their lovely mansions.

Occasionally you'd meet these hilarious celebrities at work that you instantly hit it off with. Sometimes it was magic and sometimes that magic would be so good I'd want it to spill out of the studio and into my real life. So sometimes you'd do that, you'd go out to the pub after the interview and carry on the lols. And sometimes it wouldn't be as funny then as they'd start talking about their ex or their mortgage and then you'd never see them again. But most times you'd strike up a friendship. Pete was wary of these friendships, telling me, 'You only need one good friend,' when I'd introduce him to the sixty-seventh person we'd met that day on our royal tour of Camden.

My initial years in London were a constant merry-go-round of parties, and I'd actively encouraged Pete and Eileen to come down south and let their hair down for the week. Down they'd come on their pensioner train passes and slot into whatever I was up to that week. That might be a DJ set, a day of filming something or a couple of chats with a pop star, busy but hardly WORK work. They were not getting the violins out for me, put it that way. However, it was non-stop from one thing to another to another. I'd happily bring them along to Radio 1 or T4 via a Fashion Week party or two and they used to love it, but as Eileen would say, 'We did love it but we loved the train home more.' Fair.

Eileen would be clued up via reliable mum channels like *Lorraine* on the big hitters in showbiz, but my dad was hardly Perez Hilton. Pete had a killer catchphrase: 'WHO THE BLEEDIN' 'ELL IS (insert celebrity name)?' First and most iconically used when I came home in a Marc Jacobs jacket and flung it on their couch. Pete was livid at the coat not being hung up properly, and drilled over and over and over that I 'needed to move this bleedin' ugly coat.'

I protested, 'It's not ugly, it's Marc Jacobs!'

With 100 per cent sincerity Pete replied, 'Who the bleedin' 'ell is Marc Jacobs? and why have you got his bleedin' coat? Shift it!'

His knowledge of the cultural world did not develop from there. There was the time he told me Angus Deayton was a fabulous-looking model. He meant Agyness Deyn. The time he told me Marie Caru was an excellent singer. He meant Mariah Carey. And the time I interviewed Beyoncé and excitedly told him and he responded with 'Who? Never bleedin' heard of her in me life.'

The one name he was adamant to see on his jaunts to London was Josef Sheekey. Not an actor, a pop star or the spawn of some-one famous, but a fishmonger who in 1890 was given land in Covent Garden to sell fish. Unfortunately Our Josef is no longer with us but he did leave behind quite the legacy in his restau-rant; J. Sheekey, an absolute essential for a London-bound Pete: 'It's classic. None of this trendy garbage you take me to. Let's go there.'

So off we go, it was an unwritten rule that we went with Pete as it was no-nonsense with a top-notch quality pie. So it was understood that, as much as we'd like to try a new sushi spot or some Peruvian place with a DJ, it would be SHITE, so old faith-ful Sheekey's it had to be. And to be fair to him, it was always reliably banging.

We ordered the fish pie as usual and finally, after a day of rushing around to press junkets and them joining me for TV production meetings, we got to spend some quality family time together. Eileen is doing her silent eye-raises that say, 'Oh, it's lovely here, get us!' when I get a text that makes me shriek out an involuntary gay noise.

'What the bleedin' 'ell was that? What's wrong wi'yer?' Pete said.

'Omg Fran has just sent me the maddest text,' I scream.

They put their knives and forks down and roll their eyes. 'Fran! Bloody 'ell!' Pete says.

They know her rep. Fran is Fran Cutler, a legendary Londoner who plans parties for a living. Ludicrous I know. She is this tiny but bombastic, giant-boobed cockney with a cheeky face and a dirty mouth. She swears more than an angry sailor. She is legendary on the London party scene and has been dubbed a Rottweiler in lipstick by the papers. But that's not fair. She rarely wears lipstick.

She's all 'faaack this' and 'faaaccck that', hands down one of the most brilliantly mad people you could meet. If she was written into a sitcom you'd complain she was overwritten and overacted. Apart from, she ain't acting. It's real. And hilarious.

When I arrived in London she was the gatekeeper to nights out. She did the guestlist, the invites, the afterparties, Fashion Week, festivals – you name the pie, her fingers were in it. But we didn't get off to the greatest start. I met her at the Vodafone Music Awards (no me neither) and as I sat down she promptly marched over to me and said, 'YOU! Who the fuck are you? You can't sit there, fuck off.' Since moving down from Oldham I had never met a woman like this in my life. And to be fair haven't since.

My mum and dad loved Fran because she cut through the bullshit of London and to a northerner it was warmly reassuring that someone else saw the occasional absurdity of life down here. Like Pete, she said it how it was, even when you didn't ask her to. And she, like us, loved family, always asking over the banging party whenever I arrived, 'How's yer mum? How's yer dad? Right, get fucking in and start fucking DJing!'

Her text this night was classic Fran. Direct, absurd and fun.

It read, 'Madonna is havin' a party tonight.'

'Oh Nick. No. Don't start,' said Eileen, raising her hands to her temples.

'Madonna? Party? Tonight?' My dad taking it in like he's receiving Morse code.

'YES! Madonna! Party! We have to go! Come on!' I say, trying to rally the troops.

'Nick! I'm dressed like I'm going to Sainsbury's!' Eileen protests. 'I'm not going like this!'

'We're having a pie, we're not rushing off!' Pete cried.

'You look great Mum! And Dad, we'll go after our pies,' I say.

The pies arrive and we discuss the merits of going and not going.

Pros: Madonna is there.

Cons: Eileen is conscious she's in a George at Asda coat.

Pros: no one will notice.

Cons: I do have the Breakfast show to do in about eight hours.

Pros: maybe Madonna will provide endless lols for the show.

Pros: Fran will make us laugh.

Cons: Fran will shout at us.

They can't decide and um and ahh it over.

We HAVE to go I think. I try to make analogies to show the significance of Madonna to me by speaking in Pete's language: football. This is like you meeting Rooney, I say.

Rooney? He's a bleedin' kid.

Well not Rooney then . . . Pelé.

Pelé! Madonna's not bleedin' Pelé!

Cantona?

He shakes his head and I'm out of footballers.

They sense my impatience and deep wanton Madonna need and agree we can go, after the pie of course. I agree; great plan: pie then Madonna.

I'm taken back to family holidays where I'd be desperate to wrap up dinner so I could go watch the evening entertainment in the hotel lobby. Eileen would be savouring a teaspoon-sized serving of wine in her glass: 'We can go when I finish my wine!' Back then I'd forcibly tip the wine down her neck by angling her elbow upright in a bid to get to the evening's activities. But now I felt I'd matured and so decided to opt out of spoon-feeding her the fish pie at breakneck speed. I passive-aggressively wolfed mine down, the molten prawns taking a layer off my tongue, meaning I won't taste food for a week – but worth it for Madonna.

'Calm down, I'm not bleedin' rushin' for bleedin' Madonna!' Pete said.

We wrapped up the seemingly excruciatingly long meal – no need for desserts, I thought – and off we went in a black cab to the party, just an hour or so later than the designated arrival time. It is a shit-show outside: crowds have formed of frenzied Madonna fans and movie-premiere levels of paparazzi. Shit! We're never gonna get in now, that bloody, delicious, fish fucking pie has made us late!

While cursing the pie, I usher in the Oldham OAPs, still digesting their tea, into what was beginning to feel like THE invite of the year. In all my years of parties and DJing I'd never seen Madonna in the flesh and my sense of gay panic was now sky-high. What will she be like? Will she be dancing? Who is going to be there? Omg what happens?

We go in and I'm expecting Studio 54. And it was like Studio 54.

But Studio 54 now: derelict. There was NOT a SOUL in there. What the fuck? The place was cold with air con as the disco lights spun round over no music so you could hear their motors churning, and it had all the fabulousness of a school disco.

'I rushed my pie for this? I thought you said it would be good,' Pete said with a told-ya-so smile.

Fran told us we were too early, even though we were well over an hour late.

'It's eleven o'clock,' Eileen said, 'you've got to be up at five!'

Oh God. We did rush that pie for no reason. Could've had dessert too, I thought, as I cursed the timekeeping of London liggers. Where the hell is everyone?

Fran told us, 'Kim and Kanye are here, they're coming in now . . .'

'Who?' my dad said.

'Kim and Kanye!' Fran screamed as she shoved us down at the nearest table.

'Kimunkanyer? Who's that? Never heard of her,' Pete shrugged.

'No they are TWO people, Dad. Kim is . . .' I tried to explain but too late, they were here.

Then there was this incredible moment. Kim Kardashian and Kanye West, two of the most famous people on the planet, dressed up like the Hollywood mega-celebs they are, descending into what they thought, just like I did, would be THE social event of the year. Kim steps her manicured, Louboutin-clad foot into the club and sees not Madonna, not the London glitterati but Eileen and Pete – 'Hiyaaaaa luv!' It was giving cruise ship: two OAPS from Oldham sat in an empty room with the lights still flashing.

'Blooooody 'ell, who the bleedin' 'ell is that?' Pete said in understandable shock at seeing a PVC-clad Kardashian up close and personal.

Kimunkanyer look confused. It's not for them. They turn on their heels and head back up the stairs.

Over the course of the night the room fills up and soon the place is packed with the great and good of London life. And it turns out that wasted celebrities love nothing more than talking to some random oldies. Like a dog on the Tube, everyone wanted to throw them a smile, or at least point at them. Their first interaction of the night saw, inexplicably, a manic movie star rush over to check that Eileen wasn't cold.

'Hi! Are you cold?' they asked.

Shocked, Eileen replied, 'Erm, a little chilly . . .'

The earnest movie star was keen to help. 'Oh no! Let me see if I could do something.'

'You could always pop the heating on?' Eileen replied.

The movie star was off on a mission.

'Does she work here?' Eileen asked me.

'No she doesn't,' I replied. I explained that she was Lindsay Lohan and no she's not going to have the right credentials to pop the heating on unfortunately.

'Who the bleedin' 'ell is Lindsay Logan?' Pete said, shaking his head.

She came back, failed on her mission to turn up the heating in Annabel's. Fair. Intent on monitoring my mother's core temperature, she offered to nip home to get Eileen one of her Chanel cardigans, to which Eileen replied was too much fuss and she'd survive. So brave of her. Once the party got rolling, we'd occasionally be split up and, fuelled by a carby pie, Eileen and Pete were off on one. I found Eileen in deep conversation with Mark Ronson (possibly asking him to turn the immersion on); and Pete, like a big masculine bloodhound, sniffed out the only other person willing to talk about football at a Madonna party whilst 100 gays twerked on a light-up dancefloor: Noel Gallagher.

Then the big moment. Madonna arrived. And rather than us hitting it off and becoming best friends, she kept herself to herself in the corner, surrounded by a gaggle of muscle gays. Maybe word had got out about Eileen being cold and Pete exclusively trying to start chats about *Match Of The Day*. We leave and they comment the party was 'Fine. Not worth rushing that pie for.' We make a family pact: it's pies over pop stars from now on.

That's not their only run-in with celebrity though. There was the night we went to see Kylie and were brought backstage for a meet and greet, where all of a sudden the Kylie team dissolved and it was just me, Eileen and Pete watching Kylie eat her tea in a white-linen-clad room as, you guessed it, Pete spoke about United to her and invited her over for Eileen's Sunday roast the next day.

A few years later, Pete had cocktails with Sienna Miller, who he told had a 'very 1960s face', Eileen met A$AP Rocky and told him he had fabulous teeth, she got a lift home from the theatre from Jake Gyllenhaal, and had dinner with Stella McCartney and Rihanna . . . nothing fazed them.

A January morning in 2009 meant that for all eternity Pete referred to Lady Gaga as 'me mate gaaaaah gaaahh'.

Y'see the 'rents were down in London and I had time off from my E4 responsibilities to hang out with them, bit of lunch and a trip round M&S. Even though as my dad and I would pro-test they have M&S in Manchester. Mum would insist 'THEY HAVE DIFFERENT STYLES HERE!'

While browsing our fifth rail of definitely not different styles on Oxford Street (you know, the secret shopping enclave where they keep all the exclusive M&S pieces), I got called and asked to cover an interview. Someone had dropped out and now they had no one to interview this big American star. It was less an ask and more a have-to.

Eileen got her very exclusive DEFINITELY NOT AVAIL-ABLE IN MANCHESTER M&S CARDIGAN and off we went to TV land, Eileen excited for a nosey and Pete excited not to be shopping in M&S. I think they were imagining some fab TV studios but the magic of E4 Music was made in these two tiny, crummy rooms in a multi-use office block in Notting Hill. It was, shall we say, charming. The studios had no soundproofing, so every time a truck or train went past, which it did roughly every three minutes, you'd have to stop your A-list guest mid-flow and say, 'Sorry . . . gonna have to stop you, let that train go,' then wait in silence for fifteen seconds and then say, 'OK, off you go.' They could never remember where they were with their story and we'd have to redo it all again, leading to less than perfect interviews. Oprah's back garden it wasn't.

On this particular day, with my OAP entourage, we arrive into a storm of topless dancers in DIY crop tops, flying hair extensions, backing singers doing warm-ups, American publicists with two phones, all cramping the rooms and spilling out into the hallway. My producer shouts me over, squeezing through the chaos to introduce me to the reason we are all here: newly famous and for the first time on British soil, Lady Gaga. She is roughly one foot tall and wearing a thick blond wig with a giant fringe over the eyes and full stage show make-up. A minuscule rag of skirt covers just about what it needs to and she's crouched down applying gaffer tape to some sort of *Lord Of The Rings*-style stick/prop thing and jumped up with stage school pizzaz and a 'HEY I'M GAGA'.

She confidently strode across the room, right up to my face, too close for comfort, and stared deep in my eyes. She was so close I could feel the temperature of her breath. I managed to see her face under the wiggy fringe and felt her excitement at being here, eager to perform. She felt instantly mega-famous, she felt like a star, and I was happy that we'd made the decision to ditch M&S for this.

'This is my mum and dad,' I said, introducing the semi-naked Gaga to Eileen and Pete down from Oldham for the day in their matching coats.

'Ohhh hiyaaaa . . .' my mum said with a smile that said, 'I really shouldn't be here.'

Gaga flung her arms around them and held their hands on the top and bottom like your nana does when she gives you money. Noticing their awkwardness in the midst of the chaos, she offered up her dressing room as theirs, proclaiming she didn't really need it now.

The room was alight with excitement and laughing at itself at the concept of this new DIY artist covered in duct tape with three topless oiled-up dancers straight from a New York gay club sharing a room with two OAPs from Oldham who were watching open-mouthed in silence.

Realising the humour in the situation, Gaga indulged us all. 'Daddy, am I all covered up correctly?' sticking her gaffer-taped nipples out to show him.

'Yer all right love,' he said, shaking his head and folding his arms up in stern-dad mode.

'She's gonna be freezing in that!' Eileen said, 'she's not wearing that is she? She'll catch her death!'

Hair done, tits taped up and *Lord Of The Rings* totem-pole-thing constructed, it's time for Gaga to do her thing. It's her first performance outside of the States and it's one she's evidently focused on, checking every inch of herself in the mirror to the stage. The entourage assemble and off they go en masse to the studio floor like worker ants surrounding their queen. But wait, there must be a problem: she stops in her tracks. She turns and shouts back to 'Mom & Dad' aka Eileen and Pete, suggesting they follow the Haus Of Gaga into the studio to watch the performance. We do our chat and then it's singing time. I leave the stage and see that Eileen and Pete have settled in behind the camera, eagerly watching as a dancer lies down with his feet flat in the air for Gaga to plop a keyboard on. I mean, why use a keyboard stand when you have a go-go dancer to spread their legs for you? She knocks out a flawless rendition of 'Poker Face'. I look over and Eileen has picked up the lyrics, clapping along in her Wallis coat: 'p p p p p poker face p p p p poker face' and waving her hands out front in a Charleston stylee. It's good but it's not as good as Gaga. She is going for it in an epic performance complete with complicated choreography, Freddie Mercury-style hand-clutches to the sky, headbanging, live vocals, a vocoder moment, a keyboard solo and ending on a high with a 'MA MA MA MAAHHHH' and a crescendo of crashing symbols. As is standard in a TV record, rather than rapturous applause everyone knows to stay silent, allowing the camera to pan out and collect the drama of the stage before a director yells cut and THEN we can applaud. The room falls silent as Gaga reaches the end note and stands still, panting, locked solidly and silently in her pose.

I hear a northern voice pipe up.

'Is that a bloke?'

I carry on looking forward and pray for the first time since childhood that he doesn't repeat the question. Thankfully Eileen's dagger looks have made him subside into silence.

Around this time work began to ramp up and I'd have fewer and fewer days off and less and less time up north. But one weekend I went home with my friend Aimee. Pete and Eileen loved Aimee cos she, like Fran, cut the shit. Pete loved nothing more than a sassy New Yorker with no-nonsense chat and Aimee had that by the bucketload. On the train we encountered a baying mob of middle-aged musical hooligans. They were swigging their G & Ts in a can and singing Adele songs. We told Eileen and Pete of our rowdy travelmates.

'Oooooh she's playing the Arena in town tonight,' Eileen said.

I suggest that we can go and it was like they'd won the People's Postcode Lottery, jumping out of their seats and slippers to go get ready. There was a very short list of who Pete liked in the modern world and a very long list of who he thought was shite. Thankfully Adele was on his like list. So off the four of us went.

It was March 2016 and Pete was suffering with post-chemo pains and needed to wee a lot, so would be lightly jogging to the bogs every few minutes like a pregnant lady.

We make it through 'Hello' and 'Chasing Pavements' and in and out of Adele's stand-up routine. Then she starts to talk about a friend of hers.

Lol does she mean me?

She says her friend is in the audience tonight.

Oh is this me? Aimee and I start joking – lol if it's me!

She says she hasn't seen her friend in a while.

OK lol like me, I'm listening . . .

She said she used to be really, really tight with this friend but they'd lost touch somehow.

Hey, that happened to me!

She said that her and her friend used to bumble around London trying to make it.

I mean, I did do that with her, maybe she does actually mean me?

Her discretion was over. I'm talking about Nick Grimshaw from Radio 1. Where are you babe?

OK it's me.

The lights come on and 20,000 people stare at me as I wave nerdishly back at Adele. It is a very surreal experience.

'Awww miss you babe, let's have a curry and a catch-up, I'd love that.'

I reply, 'Oh yeh lovely, I'd love that,' but she can't hear me. I do thumbs up and nod in a pantomime style so she can read my yes from the stage.

'Anyway. I miss you. This one's for you,' she says.

The opening piano chords of 'Make You Feel My Love' begin.

I look down the row to my left and see Eileen's giant green eyes glistening with held-in tears. She has an empty seat next to her and has never looked so alone.

'Where's Dad?' I ask.

'He's gone for a wee,' she says.

I turn back and as Adele begins to sing, tears stream down my face at the thought of Eileen alone. Of her spending the rest of her time with an empty seat beside her. The song isn't helping and when the strings kick in, my throat begins to ache and choke itself.

Adele sings about how the winds have changed and how there is nothing she wouldn't do to make love be felt. It's a lot. A song I've numbed myself to by hearing it and playing it thousands of times on the radio all of a sudden hits home hard like never before. Ugh fuck, everything has started to feel very real. There's a lot to unpack right there in that three-and-a-half-minute song. The sickly sweet duality of Adele's kind declaration of love and the poignancy of my dad missing it.

His cancer was incurable. And for a while I'd been ignoring it or avoiding thinking about it or maybe thinking it was going to be OK. But here was the first time that I realised that actually it wouldn't be. I sat there and cried at the thought that it would be the first of many things that he would miss. The first of many things Eileen would have to experience alone. I think that's why she cried too.

As Adele wraps up the song, me, my mum and Aimee are a mess.

Pete returns down the stairs: 'What the bleedin' 'ell is wrong wi' you lot?!' as he looks down and sees me, Eileen and Aimee soaking wet in tears. Our sad tears immediately become happy ones as we all burst into hysterics, manically trying to process the multilayered craziness of what's just happened. Adele, a girl I once knew and who used to come to my flat for an afters, then became the most famous person in the world, has dedicated a song to me, my dad has missed it cos he's suffering from incurable cancer, the song being one of the most emotional Bob Dylan songs ever, and now the cherry on the top is his hilarious nonchalance at all of it. All of that emotional build-up instantly crashed to the floor like Jenga. Eileen now crying with laughter.

It got better.

'You missed it,' Eileen said.

'Missed what?!' he said.

'Nick got a shout-out!' Eileen said, wiping away her tears.

'From who?' Pete said, looking around.

'FROM WHO?! We're at an Adele concert! She doesn't even have a second name, who do you think from? Bloody Adele!' Eileen said, no longer hysterical from crying but hysterical in disbelief.

Pete shrugged his shoulders and sipped his pint. 'Well? So what? He knows her.'

And that is reason 1001 why I love Pete Grimshaw.

12

Wellness Whilst Unwell

Deep in my mission to party, I'd failed to think about my brain. About what staying up late all night might do to a person. Back then I'd never heard of self-care or even considered doing something remotely nice for myself. Allegedly invented by Socrates in ye olden days of Greece, self-care has gone on to be THE most annoying phrase adopted by THE most annoying girls on Instagram. And now, unfortunately, I am one of them. The phrase is instantly repellent but pass the bloody amethyst and spark-up the sage, cos I love me some self-care. It doesn't come from a wanton need to post about it online, all yoga mat rolled under arm, sipping on a matcha green almond milk latte; it's an actual need, brought on by years of doing the antithesis of self-care: hardcore self-loathing. Yay! After decades of avoiding looking after myself, I now like to think of self-care as Gay Pride for my brain, a shameless acknowledgement of embracing myself for good – we're here, we're queer and we are very anxious, so let's do something about it.

For years I indulged in self-sabotage by spending a lot of time getting very drunk, not sleeping that much, ignoring all emotional turmoil, dodging vegetables and water, and convincing myself that this was *the* way to live. NEWSFLASH! It's not. Weird, I know.

After at least two decades of dehydrated destruction cast upon myself by my very worst enemy (me), I decided it was time to meet the annoying West London Self-Care Guru Girl inside of me. And I'm increasingly coming to terms with the idea of setting her free.

I've found her hard work in the past – she takes a lot of effort and energy – but over the past few years of my mid-thirties I've semi-enjoyed getting to know her more and more. I feel better about her now, I become lighter when I indulge her, calmer, brighter, all the good things. But something is still making me keep her at arm's length. She is *quite* annoying. There's something I don't trust about her. Something's up. Just like you can't be drunk all the time, can you be caring about yourself all the time? I'm sceptical of the power she might hold over me and, like any new friend, there's the worry that she's gonna upset my old (drunk) friends.

It's unnerving to introduce this new self-loving, non-drinking side of me to pals or even myself. I can sense the weighted eye-roll of disappointment when I mention 'I'm not drinking'; sometimes the disappointment becomes more than a look and their bodies involuntarily force out a long, bassy groan: 'Uuugghhhhhh,' before a 'why?'.

Although absolutely not what you want to hear when you announce you're having a sober season, it is a very valid question. Why indeed. Well, I guess drinking increasingly became more damaging to not only my overtired liver and kidneys, but also my exhausted, frazzled brain. I just can't hack it anymore. So no drinking it is, sometimes for months on end. But rather than harp on about the intricacies of my potentially decaying organs and the fact my overemotional mind takes a frequent bashing from booze-fuelled neurosis, I say, 'I just like it.'

Which is a lie. I don't *like* it. I tolerate it. I'd like to get wasted. I'd like to go out every night, it's what I thought I was built for. I don't really like standing at a party sober, it's fine at best. But what I definitely do not like is the anxiety and the fear that comes with a hangover. It was like a reversed jigsaw puzzle, starting with remembering the fear of mornings after and then working backward from there. I was left asking myself, is drinking worth it? And the current answer is no, no it's not. But I've also been asking myself about my exploration of self-care – is *that* worth it? And the current answer is . . . maybe?

So in essence, I think I'm self-care flatlining. I've literally tried it all. Juice cleanses, meditation courses, acupuncture, cold therapy, cryotherapy, actual therapy, ice baths, infrared saunas, vitamin infused drips and colonics. I've seen nutritionists, yogis, chiropractors, had ear seeds, gong baths, cupping – you name it I've done it. Some have been life-changing, some total shit. I have so many supplements that I can't close my kitchen cupboard. There's mushrooms piled on top of turmeric pills, different green algaes for smoothies and spirulina dust spilled all over my krill oil. I'm Oldham's Gwyneth Paltrow. Apart from that I have a few shelves of baked beans and the odd packet of Mini Cheddars. Well they do say don't take vitamins on an empty stomach.

Some days I take the whole lot, shocking Mesh with my ability to choke down fifteen vitamins in one gulp. Sometimes I forget for days on end before realising with a panic similar to leaving the iron on – 'OMG MY VITAMINS!' – rushing to the cupboard to down them in haste as if they're actually keeping me alive. On the days I remember them I knock them down with my morning concoction that Mesh complains 'smells like swamp' and refuses kisses or any close contact afterwards as he thinks I smell like soil. I think it's probably good to smell like soil! I blend together a heady mix of avocado, spirulina, wheatgrass, E3 Live, hemp protein powder and collagen. Yes, it is a little swampy, but I insist that *that's* the way to start your day, not in the way that he starts his: full English, curly fries and absolutely no water. Not judging, just being jealous. I now try to sneak the pills and supplements in before he wakes up as I was recently told in a very stern and serious voice:

'WELLNESS ISN'T SEXY.'

Wow. I was in shock. Am I that boring person who's obsessed with self-care? I nearly fainted and fell to the floor but that would be impossible – I have too many iron supplements rattling around inside of me to faint. He has a point though. I obviously want to be well but I don't want to be as 'mad for it' on the wellness hype as I was the booze. Going too far either way is tragic.

I do LOVE the feeling of being gluten-, dairy-, alcohol- and sugar-free but I also love with a passion:

GLUTEN

DAIRY
ALCOHOL
SUGAR

They're legit my favourite foods. They rule! However, try as I might to balance those delicious bits in my diet, I have one of those annoying personalities that cannot find actual balance. In anything. I apply the Pringles motto to all things: once I pop, I literally can't stop. So when I first discovered the benefits of #wellness, I didn't just dip my toe but face-dived into the abyss. I went from eating a diet of salt & vinegar Discos, Coronas and Marlboro Lights to requesting no apple in my green juices in case the natural sugars were too high. It all went a bit uokhun?

Being an Oldhamer, this shift was seismic, and it had a little to do with vanity and also geography. The move to London to accomplish my radio dreams meant I was exposed to a whole new way of life, a whole new wave of people that I didn't know existed: people who went to therapy and did weird things like wear SPF in the UK. If they had something upcoming like a wedding or a job on telly they'd go on a 'juice cleanse' or pop for a 'colonic'. So that's the geography side of it – London has space and a market for this type of shit that Oldham just didn't.

'Nowt wrong wi' gluten, it's good for yer,' my dad would say as we erupted into an argument about nutrition, he for gluten, me anti it, both of us unclear what it actually even is.

The other wellness prompt was vanity – growing up, the dream was radio and radio exclusively. I didn't dream of hosting TV shows, of being photographed, of being seen. Telly didn't seem to be an option for me back then, it seemed too stiff, too proper, like you had to be clean and showered and in a suit, something teenage me was never up for. I would've snatched your hand off if I was asked to do radio but when I was asked to do some TV by Channel 4 it wasn't an immediate yes. Back when I was working as an intern at MTV, I spent my days collecting coffees for people, fetching pens for bosses and trying to disguise the fact that I'd not been to bed. I was asked to do some telly for E4 Music and was initially reluctant, thinking I was saving myself for radio and that I would probably need a Trinny & Susannah-style makeover to appear on screen. I declined and carried on fetching the pens and getting the coffees, but once that contract was over I was facing joblessness, homelessness or moving back to Oldham with Eileen and Pete. After some joyless time mooching around Camden on the dole and living on Freddos, I decided to call E4 Music back. They suggested I come in for something called a screen test the very next week. You probably don't know what I looked like back then but I wasn't 'telly-ready'. My one pair of Converse were ripped through and my jeans were caked in old beer from rolling about The Hawley Arms' floor.

I turned to Collette for help. I met her in London but she was Manchester through and through, her brilliant, thick accent omnipresent across north London at that time. She was as northern as they come: warm, kind, very funny and quick-witted all while making a rollie and sipping on a brew. Having been in London longer than me, she'd already taken on this very London way of healthy living, she had become accustomed to the trappings of self-care and, like the wicked witch of wellness, knew what to do, what to take and how to take it. She got me on to stuff I can't even pronounce that would brighten my eyes naturally and debloat my face.

'Darlin', you 'ave gotta get on the juices, you wanna be glow-in'! GLOWIN'!' she said, her eyes growing in excitement as she toiled together the magical veggies.

'Beetroot, celery, cucumber, ginger, lots of ginger, it's bril-liant for you! And LEMONSSSSS lots and lots of lemons, you wanna look gawgus, you wanna wow them telly people.'

Back then I could barely afford a pint, so we invaded the house of the only rich person we knew, our pal Sadie, and got cracking on her industrial juicer. I'd barely drunk half the glass before Collette interrupted – 'YER GLOWIN'! It's the beetroot! Yer gonna look gorgeous for the telly. No carbs either. Just fish and veggies and juice,' she said, getting strict.

That weekend I was sent a loose script to learn and in between juices and lemon water I tried to read out loud in my tiny, damp flat. Sadie, the rich one with the industrial juicer, called me. She said we should go to the country to visit her friend, Kate Moss, whom I'd never met. I agreed. I packed my script and off we went, absolutely bloody starving thanks to Collette's rigorous nutritional plan.

On the way there, I start to feel nervous and as we approach the house I worry I shouldn't have come. It's this big country pad and a vintage Rolls-Royce is parked outside. 'Are you sure she wants me here?' I asked.

'Yes of course,' Sadie reassures me as she jumps out.

Kate answers chuffing on a fag and a big smile on her face. ''elllo darlin', come in! Do you want a Bloody Mary? I fancy a Bloody Mary!' she says before I take my coat off. 'Yes please,' I reply. Well Collette did say I should be drinking juices. Healthy, I think. Kate turns up the radio as Pete Doherty emerges, before the radio starts playing 'When You're Strange' by The Doors, and she cranks it up even louder til it's breaking the speaker as she splish-sploshes vodka and tomato juice into a glass for me. My nervousness dies down; she's warm and friendly, almost camp, her face breaking into little spasms as she knocks her head back cackling and talking about funny things she's seen on the telly. I tell them I'm auditioning for E4 Music and Kate asks me to run my lines for her and Pete in her kitchen. 'Oh, you're *so* going to get it!' We head off to the pub for lunch and while looking at the menu I tell them I've been nervous and worried about it, worried about how I look, and I tell them that I'm doing the Atkins. Kate nearly falls on the floor laughing.

'The Atkins? Are you joking! Oh don't be so stupid!' she guffaws as she chomps on some toast with melted butter, which she's topped with lashings of salt. 'Don't be all weird and change just cos you might be on the telly. Just be yourself, be you.'

Kate is offering up both sage advice and, more importantly, bread. I decide to take this advice and run with it, scoffing down some chunky toast as a symbol of my commitment.

Like Christ handing out his loaves, I was a loyal disciple at the church of carbohydrates. I'd never seen someone pour salt on toast and melted butter and followed suit.

I got the job a few days later and within a month I was on TV. I was off the dole and starting to 'do some bits'. The bits became more frequent and I was asked to bring some other clothes and maybe some clean shoes, or at least ones without holes in them. One thing struck me when I started – you spend an unnatural amount of time looking at yourself. I didn't even own a mirror and all of a sudden I was being plonked in a make-up chair and forced to look in one directly at myself for an hour a day. And with that you start to notice what you actually look like: you're literally being made to look nicer by a professional who paints on what your face *should* look like. It's not GREAT for the psyche. Sure, if you're toast-bingeing Kate Moss the view back ain't too shabby, but for portly, square-headed fellows like me it wasn't always too kind a reflection. You're also surrounded by exclusively good-looking people for your job – pop stars and movie stars in full drag. I started to think that maybe the bread covered in butter isn't the best for me. Maybe lager isn't the one. Maybe I'd like to not feel exhausted all day at work because I quite like my job, so maybe I should stay in the odd night.

A few months in, fuelled by vanity and wanting to look nicer on the telly, I started to do crazy London things like buy a moisturiser, or maybe I'd have a steam. Stuff 'I wouldn't have had to do for radio,' I'd complain to myself in my head. Don't get me wrong, this was still a time in my life where I relished getting blackout drunk, but the initial seeds of self-care were starting to sprout. I was in a constant battle of being sick from a hangover or sick from a vitamin drip. I'd be aching from either a full body workout or falling down the stairs of the Lock Tavern pissed out me head. I was never balanced, in harmony; it was one extreme or the other and, I must stress, both *were* extreme.

One summer, bored of the yo-yo dieting and the back-and-forth between alcoholism and Buddhism, we decided it was best to go to a juice detox centre. I was led there by my co-host and partying co-conspirator Miquita Oliver.

'Let's go,' she said. 'It is amazing for you,' she said.

There we would fix this mess once and for all; we'd go to the countryside for the week and come back looking like Cindy Crawford.

We lasted one night. I don't know what we thought was going to happen but we had fuck all to do apart from not eat. There were two activities:

1. don't eat anything.
2. drink some juice.

Not fun!

The day was spread out over three juicing moments, one at brekkie, one at lunch and a mid-afternoon one. Then came the evening's big moment: communal soup. Now, I hate soup at the best of times – for the record, it is my least favourite genre of all food.

We headed down to dinner and gathered around a long wooden table where a group of housewives sat slurping their low-calorie broth in silence and, like very hungry monks, we joined them and congregated in prayer. Our prayer was a simple one:

Dear God,
Please make us thin. Amen.

Morale was low. The next morning we woke at 6 a.m. absolutely starving and bored shitless. I don't know if you've ever tried to starve yourself on a juice cleanse but it's the most boring thing I've ever tried in my entire life. It felt like a prison sentence, except worse; they have food in prison. We realised that smoking gave us SOMETHING to do, sucking in anything we could, hoping to inhale some very-much-needed calories. As I chuffed away, wishing I could just die already, Miquita stood bolt upright.

'We're going. This isn't for us!' she exclaimed as she started packing.

'Shall we just stay one more night at least?' I asked.

'No. We're going. It's weird. We need to leave.'

I agreed and threw my fag out the window and packed up.

'What will we say?' I asked.

'Shit. What will we say?' Miquita mused.

We stood nervously in the hall with our bags packed and coats on, silently trying to concoct a plan as to why we had to flee. We ran through about ten scenarios: maybe we're sick, maybe someone is dead, maybe there is a job we've both got, or we double-booked something.

'No, no, no. Stop, we are adults. We can just leave, they don't care!' I said.

'Exactly. Let's just say that's that and we're off home,' Miquita agreed.

It wasn't that easy. The man on reception, it seemed, had experienced this before: carb-starved, panicked people wanting to escape and run round their nearest drive-thru on foot.

'We would like to check out please,' I said, voice all shaky from the fear of being told no – and a lack of a substantial meal for ALMOST a full day now.

A barrage of questions followed:

Why?
What happened?
Is there something wrong with the room?
Do you not like it here?
Is there anything we can help you with?
Surely you can't leave?
You do realise you still have to pay?

'Yes, yes, we realise that,' Miquita interrupted. 'The thing is, Grimmy's dog has gone mental.'

My eyes bolted at Miquita, confused and panicked.

'We need to leave RIGHT NOW.'

The guy looked petrified. 'Oh, of course, shall I order you a cab to the station?'

'Yes, please. It's quite urgent,' Miquita replied. The big fat liar. 'Are you OK Grim?' she asked, sounding so convincing at being sad that I thought my dog *HAD* gone mental.

I nodded and did that strong, polite smile that British people do when someone holds the door for you.

I didn't speak until we got in the cab and had made it halfway up the gravel driveway.

'Miquita!' I screamed. 'What happened to us being adults and just saying we were leaving?'

'Oh he was annoying! He wouldn't stop! I just wanted to get out of there,' she said as she scrolled on her phone nonchalantly.

We got cans of lager at the station and ripped open a packet of crisps to share on the way home.

'Hey, we tried,' she said, as we cheersed our cans and planned where we were going to go out that night. We headed to her mum Andi's restaurant, where she offered us dinner but absolutely no support. 'I knew you two wouldn't do it! What a stupid idea.'

Years later, I left Radio 1. I wanted a proper breather. Not that I'd been down a mine for fourteen years, but being on air and in constant search of content on a daily basis for that long warranted some sort of break. And not just a holiday break, a mental break. Upstairs, the old noggin was programmed to be constantly thinking of 'stuff' for things to fill the daily three-hour show with. When I left the show, I found myself still trying to make 'stuff' out of things. I'd be watching TV making notes about a funny line, or writing down something someone said in a shop, or a funny meme I saw, stuff that would be good on the show tomorrow, except there was no show tomorrow. I'd left – but my production brain still thought I worked there. I wanted it to stop. I needed to shake off that self-taught producing-for-radio brain and think about my actual life and not my on-air one. So I did something that I'd never done and block-booked out a month. A month for me. A month where I could reflect and breathe and have a think about what just happened and what I wanted to do next. I randomly decided the ideal place for this was Los Angeles. I'd been many times before and it was the per- fect balance of relaxing and productive. I'm not mad for lying around on a beach all day with nothing to do but I do like the sunshine, and LA has that, but it also has a fully functioning entertainment industry – so maybe I'd rest a bit and work a bit. Free from the in-your-face harshness of New York or London, it's a city that moves at a glacial pace, which was exactly what I was after. It is also the wellness capital of the world.

Just before leaving I got Covid and had to push it back and in that time the self-care nosedived. Over the course of my ten-day isolation period I binge-ate, binge-drank and therefore binge- piled hate on myself. Plus, obviously, I was locked in the house with a virus, missing Christmas and my family for another year, so things were not feeling too peachy. Once I get to LA I'll be all right, I thought. Unfortunately landing in California was not the magical remedy I had hoped it would be. My anxiety was sky-high and my senses peaked at the concept of being on the other side of the world. My near-white reflective skin was in shock at this sort of heat after two Boris Johnson-enforced years on Plague Island.

After a few days of not sleeping from a mixture of jetlag, feeling misplaced and an unplaceable sense of dread, I decided to take advantage of the liberal Californian laws and seek anxiety relief from a herbal high. I'd pop on some cosy Birkenstocks and smoke weed in a tie-dye shirt, smiling away my fears as I basked in the sunshine, I thought.

Imagining myself somewhere between Rihanna and Seth Rogen, I headed off in search of drugs. My stoner role models seemed to have all the qualities I was after at this point in my life; they seemed full of self-love, their inner joy oozing out of their stoned pores. Yeh! I'll do drugs just like them, I thought.

Now I must confess I am not a weed aficionado and my last spliff experience in California hadn't gone to plan. The last time I partook in some stateside spliff action was at the MTV Video Music Awards in 2010 here in Los Angeles. My very first London pal Mairead had grown from club kid to music manager and was now managing Florence + The Machine, who then were on the verge of superstardom. I'd spent the previous few years rolling around pub shows, club shows, basically all shows with a bar, and was invited along to what would be Flo's first US performance, one not to miss, and it turned out to be quite the iconic evening. In more ways than one.

2010 was a GREAT year for pop music. It felt alive, healthy and thriving, so the room was filled with the crème de la crème of pop. I'm talking Rihanna, Bieber, Eminem, Justin Timberlake,

Drake, Mary J. Blige, Katy Perry, Pharrell, even bloody Cher was there, who looked *so* much like Cher that I presumed it was someone in Cher drag and not actual Cher. It was the infamous night that Gaga wore *that* meat dress and won everything and Kanye sang, 'Let's have a toast for the douchebags' on loop for ten stunning minutes. I sat in the audience with Isa aka 'The Machine' while Florence performed on stage and cemented herself alongside those pop giants as an international megastar. I remember thinking I was in over my head and everyone was just TOO famous to take in; I was fine in a pub in Camden with contemporaries but this was something else. You're not supposed to see Cher with your very own eyes, just stood in a room, I don't think. Me and 'The Machine' decided the best thing to do was get drunk but in Los Angeles, a city obsessed with wellness, it was harder than we thought. No drinks were allowed into the auditorium, absolutely unheard of in the UK. We were aghast at the thought of having to stay sober.

'What? We just sit there and watch the show without drinks?' we moaned to the barman.

'A gig without a drink? Not even a beer? Can't we just take in a beer? Surely a beer is OK? It's hardly alcoholic!' we argued.

He didn't budge. 'You can drink at the designated drinking areas, not inside watching the show.'

'Ugghhhh! Fine! We will drink here during the boring songs and boring awards and rush back for the good ones,' we decided. Plan sorted.

We sat for Rihanna and Eminem. RAN to the bar during a pre-recorded Bieber section. Rushed back to our seats for the unmissable Drake and Mary J. Blige number and took several shots at the bar for the absolutely missable Usher medley of 'DJ Got Us Fallin' In Love' and the heinous 'OMG', a song so god-dam awful that it's almost good. We rushed back for Florence's song and back to the bar to down a bottle of white wine while Bruno Mars and B.o.B sang about aeroplanes. And by the time Kanye ended the show with 'a toast for the douchebags', we'd partaken in one or two toasts already and were definitely acting like douchebags, the anthem we deserved. We swung by the afterparty, where Flo and I were DJing and Florence skipped and flew around the room aloft compliments from the world's most famous pop stars. About fifteen minutes into our set, Flo had an update: 'I'm going to Drake's studio now, come when you've finished DJing,' she said. Casual.

Now left alone to DJ, I calmed the nerves by sampling the delights of the free white wine and chugged it down merrily as I did a terrible job at mixing any records at all, half my fault cos of the nerves, half the white wine's fault.

Once I was done I headed to meet the gang at the studio. Florence was there, Mairead too, Rob and Isa from the band, all sitting around on a sofa while Drake took an office wheelie chair in front of a mixing desk. I was a little nervous about being there but Drake's lovely kind face and 10/10 hosting skills made me feel as welcome as anyone: 'Take a seat, do you want a drink?' He played some tunes and Flo wailed along as someone passed around a comedy-sized cartoon-like spliff.

'Ooooooh yeh why not, a spliff with Drake in California, what could go wrong?' Ignoring the prior twelve hours of white wine abuse. I decided the icing on *this* messy cake should be weed. I chuffed down on it and smiled at Drake, his big almond eyes and wide smile reassuring, all calm and serene and comforting, like a rapping golden retriever. The music continued and I went silent, I started to sink more and more into the couch, it was the first time I think I've ever been quiet when awake. I was content for maybe sixty seconds. Then the weed met the wine. And they didn't seem to get on. The room started spinning, the former still, calm studio now moving pretty fast, as the glass walls appeared to zoom past my eyeballs like a bullet train. I needed Drake's eyeballs again! I tried to focus on his kind face, like a deity that would drag me out of this self-created hell I'd drunk and smoked myself into. His kind face wasn't working this time.

I was throwing THE biggest whitey ever.

I stood up sharply. Bad move. A chorus of 'Uh-oh . . . are you OK?' rained down on me from the room. I was in a bad way and thought the best thing to do was leave. I stepped a foot outside and proceeded to projectile-vomit for what felt like thirty minutes. Ugh. At least I didn't puke in there, in front of Drake, imagine the embarrassment.

Happy I'd got away with it, I stepped back in, pale and smelling slightly of vom. The room erupted in a fit of laughter. How did they know? I wondered. I looked up to see a CCTV screen showing the exact location of the vom incident. I hadn't gotten away with it, I'd had it live-streamed to the studio.

Now, back in LA in 2022, I decided to park that horror story in the dark depths of my mind – maybe *this* time the weed won't do that to me. Maybe *this* time it will allow me not to puke but to become at one with myself. Plus I'd stopped drinking. It was probably the wine's fault.

With Dr. Dre's 'smoke weed every day' on loop in my head I decided to act upon this seemingly solid piece of advice and head off in search of the green stuff. Now this is 2022 in California; finding weed is not the seedy drug deal you'd imagine, it has all the drama and illegality of going to buy a loaf of bread. The palm-tree-lined streets are filled with shops with flashing neon signs inviting you in to light up and chill the fuck out. I opted for a shop on Santa Monica Boulevard in a nice part of town that looked as clean and modern as the Apple Store, hoping *this* would be the cure to my chaos.

'Heyyyyy, welcome to the store, are you having an amazing day?' My welcome was warm and confident, the staff in uniform holding iPads and wearing matching polo shirts.

'Yes, er, well, kind of . . .' I was absolutely clueless about weed sold in a store that was like Warhammer for weed nerds. 'One marijuana spiff please,' I said.

'What exactly are you after? What kind of high? Do you like sativa or more of a THC? Or maybe a THC/CBD blend? Will you be smoking it at night? Or like, more of a like, daytime vibe?' the guy said.

Realising I was very much out of my drug-taking depth and not the cool Californian I thought I'd be, I just told the truth. 'Well, I don't smoke weed and I have chronic anxiety, so I need something that's going to be super-chill and take the edge off my mental head.'

'Right, got it. First of all, so sorry to hear that, I get anxiety too, this will REALLY help. OK let's try this one . . .'

I was led over to look at a box of pre-rolled tiny little spliffs in a flowery, cute box. They looked like little baby spliffs a toddler could probably smoke. 'This is maybe good for you, super-chill, super-mellow, really nice to chill to.'

'Will I freak out? I don't want to freak out.'

'No, it's super-light, great for anxiety and it's just gonna relax you a little,' he said.

Perfect, I thought. So I got the box of four pre-rolls and walked out, past the array of people in there all picking up their drugs like they were in Tesco getting bits for tea.

I got home and headed up to the roof, and with the image of a relaxed Rihanna in my head I sparked it up in the sunshine. I felt nothing.

'Waste of bleeding money that was,' I said out loud in disbelief.

I waited five minutes and sparked it up again, this time choking down on it like Dot Cotton. I started to feel something this time. The edges of the green trees popping up into the blue sky started to blur, the palm trees swaying in the light wind seemed to go in slow motion. Am I . . . high?, I thought to myself as I closed my eyes and felt the cannabis flow round my body, the heady mix of sunshine and weed flooding my brain with serotonin. And for a mini second I felt the weightlessness of being anxiety-free.

Then something happened. I opened my eyes and I didn't like it. Everything started melting, the floor unfolding and collapsing outwards, the building across the road falling in like those shit-scary bits in *Inception*. I needed to focus on something, so I picked up a magazine and could see my hand moving in slow motion, like when Keanu dodges bullets in *The Matrix*. I could see in seconds. FUCCCKKKKIN' 'ell that bloody idiot in the shop has sold me some mental chronic, THIS IS NOT RELAXING.

I needed to get inside. I stood up and staggered my way to the stairs feeling like I was on a moving boat and could fall off the side of the building at any moment. In my quest for relaxation, I was starting to feel the opposite and could sense the dreaded panic creeping in. I started pulsating and my jaw began to lock. 'SHIT, I'm having a panic attack,' I said to Mesh.

'Just breathe,' he said.

'I AM FUCKING BREATHING,' I replied in the least Californian relaxed tone ever.

I started to pace and the panic doubled, the physical symptoms causing my brain to freak out more, a vicious out-of-control circle of self-torture. Previous panic attacks had made me need to seek medical attention, so now I was hell-bent on calling an ambulance.

'I'm having a panic attack, I'm going to have a heart attack, I'm going to die,' I screamed, the weed here *REALLY* doing its job of helping my anxiety. Not.

In shock at my vibrating, locked jaw, heavy breathing and crazed eyes, plus never having witnessed me in full panic mode before, Mesh agreed.

He typed in a number on his phone. I saw it was 119.

'It's 911! Not 119! You're trying to trick me! Just call one!'
The paranoia now joining the fun party upstairs in my brain.

'I'm not! You're stressing me out, I got it wrong!' he cried out,
then called 911 and got through.

'Hello, I need an ambulance, my boyfriend is having a panic
attack,' he said.

'Has he taken drugs, cocaine? Heroin?' they asked.

'He smoked some weed,' Mesh replied.

'Ooookaaaaaayyyy?' the operator replied. The eye-roll was
almost audible down the line. 'Hmmmm, some weed,' they said.

Now I must explain, this panic attack was bad. It was the first
one I'd had in two years, the previous one being in Namibia in
the back of a doctor's car when I'd genuinely nearly kicked the
bucket. So this was my brain's last memory of a panic attack and
I was magically and unwillingly transported back to the scariest
time of my life, the muscle memory of which was terrifying. Just
like the one in Namibia, it had leaked from my brain and now
gone physical, and I was shaking and fitting uncontrollably.

The ambulance pulls up outside and through the frosted glass
I can see something's not right. I open the door and see it's not
an ambulance but the fire brigade. 'Hey, we're here to help.'

'WTF! Why are the firemen here, is there a fire?' I screamed
in pure confusion; the only fire, I thought, was the one in my
cranium, burning itself to the ground.

Now, in an NHS-free country they don't send an ambulance
out, cos someone has to fork out about eight grand for that luxury. So instead they send out emergency services in whatever
vehicle is easiest, which on this occasion was some firemen.

Makes sense in hindsight. At the time it doubled down on my craziness and I felt more confused and at sea than ever before, stepping a toe into full psychosis now, not believing they were real and thinking they and Mesh were tricking and coercing me in some way.

'No, you're not real! I don't believe you!' I screamed.

'Well, we're real and you're fine,' they said. They opted not to take me to hospital and said if I wanted to go then I should get an Uber down there.

Our friend Ed offers to drive us and we squeeze into the back of his Audi TT. All wild-eyed and batty, I scream and shout from the backseat, 'Just get me there, you're going the wrong way, are you sure you know what you're doing? What are you doing?!!' to sweet lovely sober Ed. Apologies Ed.

We got to the hospital and I was crying out that I'd lost it and would never be the same again. By now I was in deep dark paranoia, not believing anyone or anything to be real. 'Do you have insurance? No? You don't? OK fill in your credit card details,' they said coldly with not an ounce of care for the top-tier panic I was experiencing. I held off handing over my credit card, with murmurs in the waiting room that an ambulance cost $8,000 a journey, the thought of paying thousands of pounds for them to give me some Pringles and a full fat Coke was a sobering thought. As I sat in the lobby of A&E and took in my surroundings, Mesh decided to call my long-suffering yoga teacher Nadia, to whom I turn when the anxiety strikes. She's zen, present and grounded, with sound advice and a calmness I could only dream of. Now when I say 'yoga teacher', I mean I go about once every six months when my rigor mortis is at its peak, and she forcibly makes my stiffened body fold in on itself. I leave thinking I'm an actual yogi. Nadia was the right call to make; she told me to breathe and leave. She grounded me and I was able to partake in a practice I'd been taught called five, five, five – counting five things you can see, five things you can hear and five you can feel. The aim is to bring you out of your mental head and back to Earth. I saw five people in more intense situations. I heard five people crying. I felt five kinds of stupid. I upped and left.

I left feeling relieved, like when your plane lands after turbulence. I was no longer drowning in the grasp of fear and I was exhausted, my body softening after five hours of lockjaw and spasming muscles. As I sat silently in the back of Ed's car on the way home feeling like how Uma Thurman looked in *Pulp Fiction*, I thought hard about what had happened. My quest to be at peace with myself was a flop. The weed did NOT turn me into the calm being that I thought it would. Maybe I was simply not meant to be calm. Maybe I was incapable of being at peace with myself. Maybe I was wired funny and maybe I just ran on anxiety and adrenaline. Or maybe you just shouldn't buy drugs and smoke them? Either way, I could strike one thing off my self-care to-do list: goodbye marijuana, thanks for making me lose my mind.

Thankfully everyone I know in LA is also insane, so I rang round to see what I could do to help my fried brain. They all chipped in with new-age health treatments; some were hot, some were cold, some were very cold then very hot, it was an overwhelming smorgasbord of wellness. I headed to Remedy Place on Sunset Boulevard, which looks kind of like a manly dark gym, but instead of equipment and gym bunnies high on testosterone, it's adorned with giant crystals and you're welcomed by a female trio of wellness warriors, serving up floral and cumin teas to aid the nervous system.

I glug down a litre of tea and cut to the chase.

'I've got anxiety. Bad. Need wellness.'

'You have so come to the right place, we are going to fix all of that,' they almost sing in their Californian accents.

'What do I need then?'

'We offer a variety of treatments for anxiety—'

'I'll take them all, one by one,' I hastily say.

Within minutes I'm stripped naked and asked to replace my former clothes with a wraparound brown towel miniskirt, fluffy Ugg slippers and some earmuffs, and shown by one of the wellness warriors a fridge-freezer like you'd see at a big Asda.

'Get in then,' she says.

'Erm. What is it? What does it do?' Only asking this now, semi-naked and about to commit.

'It's going to reach minus 135 degrees and you're going to feel amazing, it's three-point-five minutes long, would you like a song?' she says.

I get in and spend the next three and a half minutes trying not to die in this sub-freezing temperature and distracting myself from the blistering cold by pretending to be a pop star and lip-syncing to 'Tears In The Club' by FKA Twigs.

Once over it was as if someone had slapped me round the face, a hard, COLD slap round the face. After a few anxious weeks, it was the remedy I needed; I started to feel back in my body and, more importantly, out of my restless head. Next up was a realigning acupuncture session before an hour locked in what looked like a coffin for some oxygen. While in there I thought about my dad and what he would make of this and I was uncontrollably laughing my ass off. If only the man who was OUTRAGED at me having a few glasses of water a day could see me now, spending my hard-earned cash on another freely and readily available element: air. He would be beside himself.

As ridiculous as it sounds, I keep up my new LA weekly routine of being frozen, being locked in a hyperbaric oxygen chamber and being pricked with tiny needles. This plus some exercise and absolutely no alcohol, means I start to feel positive again. The black heavy dog clogging up my mind has been replaced with an upbeat and ambitious chihuahua chomping at the bit for life. But whose life *is* this? Not one I recognise. One of no alcohol, no parties, no late nights, no hangovers, no dread, but a life of meditation, exercise and eating right, one of taking vitamins, of herbal teas and self-help books. Yes I know it's good for me but it's SO annoying to me. I don't want to be *that* guy that's asking if there's caffeine in the pudding, or avoiding a party to protect my own self. Yuck!

As I head back to London, I'm struck by what a rollercoaster of self-care and self-hatred I've been on. The two feed into one another, fighting to be the top dog. I start thinking about my life back in London, and all that wellness and self-care advice

I'd consumed over the years, and which ones had weight and which ones I should sack off. And it's then that I remember that day back at Kate's and what I learnt at her country house; two things she taught me that I'll remember forever. One is that we should keep reminding ourselves that we're enough, that when we're striving for some success or acceptance and think that changing in some way may help, forget it. Just be yourself, be you. And the other is the fact that bread and butter is always better with salt. Two self-care practices I'll take to the grave.

13

Exiting a Dream

Saying I was leaving Radio 1 was great. It was like attending your own funeral but better. I got to hear eulogies from those I knew and, even better, those I didn't. It was a rare experience – like being dead but alive enough to enjoy all the expected, glorious attention and gorgeous flowers. Also, I wasn't actually dead so really there was no downside. Apart from the death of my childhood dream of getting to Radio 1. That dream was dead. It was a funny old day and the first time I thought to myself, *Maybe people actually liked me on the radio, and maybe I was OK at it*. It was also my last day. Classic. But one big question: what now? It's all I'd ever thought about and now it was done.

I started the Breakfast show in 2012 just after moving house and buying a dog. And now in the summer of 2021, I left Radio 1 during a house renovation. Change, it seemed, came in waves, seeping into all parts of my life, not just the broadcasting bit. The house was a mess so we were demoted to the spare room for these turbulent few weeks of summer. I woke up the day after my final show in the spare bedroom full of boxes. It was a hot August morning and sunlight flooded the room through the orange velvet curtains, giving the room the sort of lighting you might imagine a womb would have. Our regular bedroom is on the other side of the house where the sun doesn't rise and the poetic irony of the sunlight waking me for a new dawn of a new era of my life wasn't lost on me. I've never been woken by the sun's warm glow in our house and it felt poignant that today of all days was the first time I experienced it. I smiled for fifteen minutes, staring at the orange-hued ceiling, revelling in an almost ecstatic level of contentment. Even the towering cardboard boxes looked beautiful in this light. I turned to smile at Mesh and silently and semi-hungoverly felt the weight of what this dream had meant to me. I lay there and thought about what it had meant to my family, to my friends, my colleagues, and what it meant to strangers who had listened. My phone was flooded with messages and I cried as I learnt of the moments in their lives that I had soundtracked. For a lot of my Radio 1 years I'd been living through times where I wasn't really there for myself, so it was odd hearing that I had been there for strangers. That I made their mornings easier or made their ears prick up at the sounds of their now-favourite band. It was a lot to process. I thought about what Little Me would have thought of Bigger Me leaving the dream gig. I thought I'd made Little Me proud, and wondered what to do next. Little Me would have thought thirty-seven was ancient and life was nearly over anyway, so I should probably just die.

The radio dream started way back in my pre-teen youth. I've tried before to pinpoint what it was exactly that made me believe in radio so much. I guess it came from being desperately bored in Oldham; not being the centre of the universe at school meant I had to get my kicks elsewhere. I wasn't Queen B in the playground, so I found occasional companionship in Bill and Joan across the road. Bill and Joan were like two Oldham versions of Donatella Versace. Tanned skin like worn orange leather, both engulfed by an ever-present fog of fags. They had a funky little 70s bungalow and I thought they were fantastic. When I got bored of playing alone inside, I'd cross the road and go and knock on their door as if they too were pre-teens looking for something to do. (They couldn't have been further away from being pre-teens; they were at least eighty). I'd sit with them, watching telly as they smoked, and Bill would show me the tomatoes he'd grown as Joan gave me a bowl of ice cream, and I'd look out of the window and wave at Eileen and Pete enjoying some peace without me in the living room.

Bill and Joan were not an anomaly. I've always sought friendship in the most unlikely of places; Little Me also befriended every elderly couple on holiday, and of course I had to be present at all of Eileen and Pete's dinner parties. I didn't realise it at the time but these elderly interactions gave me a superpower – I learnt to talk to almost anyone. And when my dreams of being a rock star had started to die around age eleven after realising I couldn't sing and didn't have any other musical prowess, I decided on the next best thing: radio. Like Bill and Joan, radio had also become an analogue friend to me. We were a one-telly household with no Sky TV, so a radio up in my room gave me some freedom, some choice, some alternative universe from the near-nightly episodes of *Corrie* being blasted into the lounge. It was an (audio-only) window into another world, one I so desperately craved.

Even before I fell in love with radio for the music it gave me, I had an emotional run-in with it, which triggered something inside of me. One weekday morning, I sat with Eileen in her blue Ford Fiesta. We'd parked up but neither of us were able to leave the car; we were sucked into a story. A love story. It was Simon Bates's iconic mid-morning feature 'Our Tune', where a listener would write in and tell a tale about a special song and dedicate it to a special person in their life. I must have been no older than eight and I was totally caught up in this stranger's business. Me and Mum sat on the edge of our seats watching the radio like in wartime, edging closer to catch every last feeling from someone having their heart read out on air. I remember smiling up at Mum and seeing that she was also moved by these words. That right there was it. It was more than the song, more than the story; it was the shared experience.

I was addicted. I wanted to listen to more stories and more people and hear why a song moved them enough to write a letter and have the world hear it. In our house music was vital and, as I got to secondary school, my need to hear and consume stories became vital too. Bedtimes saw me listening to John Peel on the worn wooden floor of my bedroom as I flicked through my *NMEs* and learnt about The Fall from John. I loved the intimacy of the show. It felt warm, messy and human, like it was just me listening. I genuinely thought that I'd discovered John Peel and proudly told a schoolfriend of this funny old man that plays mad songs at night-time. I was then told that he was one of the most famous DJs ever. Right. But he felt like a friend and I leant into the irregular beats and flows of the music he played, sometimes, charmingly, at the wrong speed.

Daytime radio on the school run was a daily row over Radio 2 (Mum) and Radio 1 (me). I'd flick between the two, driving Eileen mad as she attempted to drive. She loved Terry Wogan but I argued he sounded like a pirate reading a poem, and longed for the hungover voices of Zoe Ball and Sara Cox.

By the time I was doing my GCSEs I was a firm Radio 1 mega-fan, hanging off the every word of Sara Cox and Producer Megan as they soundtracked the years where I started to think about life after school. I could do this, I thought. Sara was just what I needed then; she was live and loose, a proper raver, sounding brilliantly batty and just the right amount of rowdy. Like John, she got the day or time wrong from time to time, and I loved feeling that both of them were real people being broadcast into my tedious life. Their imperfections were inspiring to a self-doubting teen like me.

I started to listen more and more and, like I had with dogs and Ancient Egypt, I became obsessed. I felt I had to be loyal, so didn't stray from Radio 1 ever. It had taught me so much – how could I? It was here I learnt about clubs all over the world, heard about Fabric, was introduced to breakbeat by Annie Nightingale and experienced Sonar Festival sat at home. I learnt the names of all the clubs in Ibiza, the DJs and the subgenres of house music. It was a vital cultural tool in teaching me all I wanted to know about life outside of Oldham, an array of worldly madness beamed right into my suburban bedroom. Soon Zoe Ball, Chris Evans and Sara Cox became demigods to me. They were fun, accessible, witty wreck-heads who were like no one I'd ever seen or heard before, and I wanted in.

I'd never imagined myself in an actual job, being an accountant or a lawyer like my dad wanted me to be. I didn't want to do one of these proper jobs and once I got to doing my A levels I had a very specific vision. I didn't just want to be on the radio somewhere. I didn't want to just be at Radio 1. I wanted to host the BBC Radio 1 Breakfast show. And that was that.

My focus was laser-sharp, not even attempting to allow my brain to think about working elsewhere or getting 'a real job'.

Not in a cocky way; I didn't dare say it out loud but I also had no doubt in myself. It was going to happen. And years later when it actually did, I had to fake shock at it materialising. But I wasn't shocked, I knew it was coming. While the news of my hiring confused and upset Chris Moyles fans, it made sense to me that I got the job, because I'd been pretending I already had it for a decade and a half. 'Can you believe it?' people asked. Of course I can believe it, I had to. It was all I had to believe in.

For all my insecurities in life, my teen angst, wondering where to put my arms in a photo or how to stand at a school disco, I had full self-belief in what I wanted to do. I've said before it was a dream of mine, but it wasn't a dream. Dreams can be blurry and trippy, falling in and out of focus, getting lost in their own distortion. But I had crystal-clear vision on the Radio 1 Breakfast show. It was less a dream, more a calling; if anyone could chat absolute shit all day with encyclopaedic knowledge of every pop music video ever, go out all night and live to tell the tale and chat to endless strangers, it was me. I had to do it. I just didn't want to say it out loud.

Pete on the other hand was intent on me being a business-man of some sort. And my college careers questionnaire came back, inexplicably, with the suggestion of Funeral Director. Maybe the next dream to conquer? 'Grim Funerals' does have a ring to it.

One Sunday afternoon, procrastinating about my college work, I went and sat downstairs with my brother's girlfriend at the time, Liane. Liane worked in design, had an Apple Mac com-puter and used to work at the Hacienda, so naturally I thought she was a living legend. I half-arsedly told her, full of hesitation and angst, that I wanted to host Radio 1's Breakfast show.

'Well, what's the problem?' she asked, sensing my reluctance.

'Well, it's hard, isn't it,' I moaned.

'Why is it hard?' she asked.

'Well, it's like being an astronaut or a footballer, isn't it?' I said.

'Yes. But people are astronauts and people are footballers,' she said.

Her words struck me. It seemed impossible, it seemed not doable. How depressing that sixteen-year-old me had already tried to talk myself out of it. I couldn't be a footballer, I couldn't be an astronaut, but I could drink complimentary drinks side of stage at a festival! I started declaring it out loud to family and friends and applying everywhere and anywhere for experience. I got little response and many firm NO's. But I never lost faith, I knew radio was going to happen for me. And it needed to – I had no backup plan.

It happened once and for all one evening in 2007, when I popped in to see Annie Mac on her new Sunday-night show. I'd met Annie a couple of years before at Glastonbury when I was working in Manchester at a company called Red Alert, where I was assisting a team of music pluggers. Their job was to get the tunes made by artists on the radio by building relationships with people at the stations. I started working there while I was at uni and then when I failed my degree miserably, they happily took me on full time.

Radio was king here, blasting out all day. It became my daily one-man mission to get radio to notice us. My mum and dad thought this job was MAD. But I loved it, listening to music then calling round radio stations all day, going to gigs, clubbing, festivals – everything I'd previously written off as the sesh was now actually work. It was during one of my 'work' trips to Glastonbury that I met Annie. She was on the radio just one night a week back then, on a Thursday, and played Erol Alkan and Tiga remixes. I was mad for clubbing and it was literal music to my ears. Really good noisy music. The Glastonbury meeting wasn't as professional as I'd have liked. I can't remember exactly what happened, but it was raining and I was wearing some fake Versace wraparound sunglasses as a joke and was mortified thinking back after meeting her that I'd not taken them off. I told Annie I wanted to be a Radio 1 DJ too aaaaaand I can't remember anything else cos Glastonbury.

A few years later, once I'd moved to London, we met again, in the Hawley. We hit it off and she told me about this new show she was going to do and how they wanted a co-host of sorts. Obviously I assumed she was talking about me and was sold. The weekly show was to be called Switch – God knows why – and was being made to soothe the Sunday-night fear felt by students the world over, to soften that end-of-the-weekend feeling.

It sounded perfect. As a kid the Sunday-night trigger of the *Heartbeat* theme on the telly used to boil my blood: FUCKING HEARTBEAT, I'd think, channelling my anger at having to go back to school deep into poor Nick Berry. HERE HE IS THE BASTARD WEEKEND-RUINER! Those nights for me felt lonely, dreading the five days ahead and getting back into character for school, putting on the armour that any soft lad would have to before the onslaught of the coming week. That pre-school dread had hung around for years and Switch was to be the antidote.

I was asked to prepare some bits that had happened to me that week and go in for five minutes to do a weekly 'what I've been up to' segment with Annie. I got there and Producer Megan – of Sara Cox fame – was to be my first producer. For a radio nerd like me it was like meeting Elvis. I had to refrain from getting a photo with her for MySpace. I chatted about new bands I'd seen and then, in a flash, it was all over and I was out of there. I remember crying as I travelled in a cab over Battersea Bridge, the fairy lights blurring in my wet eyes because the radio manifestations had finally come true. I was asked to come back the next week, this time for a twenty-minute slot, and before long Annie and I were co-hosting the show together.

We felt it was our mission to make the end of the weekend as fun as possible; we wanted it to feel chaotic and we achieved this by doing absolutely no prep whatsoever. Tucked away in the Sunday-night slot it was a slice away from the mainstream Radio 1 shows – it felt anti-establishment and anti-parent, as though the kids were taking over the school. It was completely listener-led and its weird name meant it felt like a secret club, just like the radio I had fallen in love with as a kid.

Switch was the perfect introduction to broadcasting for me, as it was absolute nonsense. Annie and I could be a mess, both sonically and visually, and we'd do long rambling links like two hungover pals in the pub. It was exactly what Radio 1 was to me in a show: wild, fun, lawless and your parents would hate it. It cured my Sunday scaries for a time, redefining what the night should feel like. And not just for me; I'd make my flatmates wait up for me to finish the show and we'd have a DIY wrap party of Coronas, crisps and cigs. (I worked two hours a week and thought that I needed a reward.)

Over the years I've learnt to prepare for shows, but back then it never crossed my mind. My only pre-show plan was: can Annie pick me up on the way? Annie lived west and I was on her way to work, about fifteen minutes away from Radio 1, so she'd pick me up en route, arriving at 6.50 p.m. with a cool ten minutes to spare for our 7 p.m. start time. Then we'd saunter in laughing about last night and just carry that on once we got on air. We had no airs and graces, no plan, no radio voice – sometimes no voice at all – and off we'd go for two hours.

It was no shock to Annie that sometimes my Sunday pick-up point would be a pub. Or sometimes it would be from a friend's house, where I'd be having a little post-roast nap and I'd have to be prodded awake and doused in Lucozade to get me going. One of my fav diversion stories for Annie was to Highgate one time to pick me up from the newly bought (and still derelict) home of Kate Moss. Kate had invited us round for a nosey after a roast, and a motley crew of guests were there to take a gander and have a glass of wine in the garden. While we sipped wine and talked, over the heads of my friends I saw Kate's neighbour from a few doors down on his balcony wearing a white dressing gown. Playing up, I jokingly waved with both hands like an SOS for attention, shouting 'COME ON OVER!!' He actually did.

He turned out to be George Michael.

Now Annie had no idea what she was about to walk in on; I'd just given her the address and no other information. So when she arrived at Kate's house to see the scene she was open-mouthed, her face saying 'omg wtf George Michael?' Imagine, ten pissed-up people in the garden and George Michael sauntering around. It got especially weird for Annie when George clocked her as she arrived: 'You're Annie Mac?? From Radio 1?!

A confused and bemused Annie was then led to a seat by George, who waxed lyrical about the merits of raving while playing her some new techno he'd got into on his phone. He's still in his white dressing gown by the way, but now with sunglasses on. Annie and George sat at a little white iron table and chairs chatting for a bit, until Annie signalled it was time to go do some work. Annie got (a now quite merry) me into her car and we arrived at the studio with minutes to spare as per usual, pumped up on adrenaline fuelled by sweet George's star power.

Annie was the most important teacher. She never preached but I watched avidly as she rode the aeroplane-like desk to fly the good ship BBC. She encouraged my craziness, the messiness, and she listened intently with her giant caring eyes you could fall into. It could've been scary there, unleashed on air at the age of twenty-three, but being with Annie was like being hugged. I felt safe and I longed for those Sunday-night mad dashes at sunset so we could be together. She held my hand through those first few years, allowing me to find my feet, mess up and be myself, bonding over hangovers and a dedicated obsession with what we were looking forward to eating later. Annie and I became firm friends fast. She was and still is everything you'd want in a friend: she listens with full ears and an even fuller heart, she has a depth of expertise across life, she is a doer, an inspirational go-getter who you can WhatsApp as you cross any bump in the road. She remains constant in my life and although I have hundreds of things to thank Radio 1 for, top of the list is my friendship with Annie.

The other great thing about the Sunday-night Switch job was that Eileen and Pete got off my case. In fact, they were over-joyed; they didn't have MTV or E4 at home so didn't know what it was – but Radio 1 they had heard of, mainly from me harping on about it for bloody years. And it was the three letters in front of Radio 1 that got my dad going: B B and C.

'Finally, a proper job!' he said.

Well sort of – the *Today* show it was not. While they thought I'd grown up overnight and become a vital BBC broadcaster, I was in fact spending my nights hanging out of my arse and mak-ing up songs with N-Dubz or encouraging guests to put their face in a bowl in a game imaginatively called Face In A Bowl. Emily Maitlis was not shaking. We played T2's 'Heartbroken' every week, and got Chipmunk to open his GCSE results live on air (I think he did all right).

I didn't get it at the time but this lawless nonsense with no parameters allowed me to be myself on air. Radio went from being a childhood obsession to something bigger; it became a therapeutic weekly practice and I became more confident in myself with each passing week. It gave me acceptance. It made me feel anchored to me, employed to talk my shit, and, on the days I was feeling confident, the more me I was, the more fun the show was, the more praise I got. It was validation. I was lucky that I would leave work feeling better and happier than when I arrived. All I needed was the attention of an internation-al A-list pop star and millions of listeners. Sometimes even that wasn't enough and I'd whine to myself on the way home from my childhood dream job that nobody likes meeeeee.

After a couple of years of pissing around on Sunday nights there was to be a change. Annie left me for prime-time: Friday night's mega dance show. She was to be the gatekeeper opening up the weekend and I was to fly solo closing it on a Sunday. At the same time I was also asked to do Weekend Breakfast, which of course I snatched their hand off to do. But ouch, I really didn't think that one through. Weekend Breakfast meant a 5 a.m. alarm, every Saturday and Sunday morning, and for 24-year-old me, 5 a.m. was around the time I'd maybe start calling it a night.

When my first weekend morning show came around, I knew the station bigwigs would be listening in and I wanted to impress, to do something other shows would talk about. So I got Adele in the Live Lounge. Great idea, right? Wrong. I didn't get her in there to sing with the voice that broke a million hearts and sold a million more records. No, no, I got her to answer the phones. I got Adele to be the receptionist. In an ill-fated feature called The Celebrity Pro Phone Answerer. Maybe not the best idea to use one of the finest voices of our generation to basically be my assistant. The next time Adele came on my show she had sold over 36 million records and I thought we should actually let her in the studio this time.

It may come as no surprise to you that I didn't last even a year on Weekend Breakfast. I was moved to night-times to host 10 p.m. to midnight, Monday to Thursday, the slot that John

Peel had held for those evening hours that captivated my teenage ears. I mean, I was nocturnal, so it made sense for both me and the BBC.

Daytime radio had bigger audiences, but evening shows felt intimidating in a different way; the DJs on air were musical experts confidently passing judgement on genres and writing off artists with a 'nah heard it before' in the very scary 'specialist office'. This cooler office was where Zane Lowe, Annie Nightingale, Gilles Peterson and Mary Anne Hobbs would all hang out. I was conscious they thought I was an idiot from T4. Mainly cos I was an idiot from T4.

I loved this show though. The regular nightly slot was something to get my teeth into and I could fall in love with the flow of a daily practice, like radio yoga.

I held an open-door policy for guests and never kicked them out, so sometimes you'd have a guest popping in for ten minutes if they were passing and hanging around till the end of the show, taking over with their own selections. The studios were right by Oxford Circus, so you'd get all sorts of waifs and strays coming by for a hang-out; some famous, some not, but both would make it on air, and, even though it was work, it started to feel like a legitimate place for friends to stop by for a drink and to say hello. I wasn't under the watch of management as they'd be – rightly – asleep at 11 p.m. on a Tuesday, so we'd get up to all sorts of nonsense.

Beth Ditto would come in and wreak havoc, dropping unflushable Maltesers down the toilet, smearing the walls with chocolate and trying to start the rumour that it was all Jo Whiley. It was a nightly hoorah and by the time the clock struck twelve there'd be a merry gang of artists, their label reps and one or two of my pals all gathered in the studio. I'd end the show at midnight and we'd all roll off for another night on the tiles. It was a wonderfully free time where the night became my friend and I became slowly more averse to daylight.

Then one morning I woke up to a text from my agent Caroline. She wanted me to meet Big Boss Ben and it had to be tomorrow morning. It seemed urgent. As you may have guessed, Ben was our Big Boss, hence the name, and was referred to as Big Boss Ben both on and off air. The name implies that he was scary but he wasn't; he was disarming and kind, but nevertheless still very much our BIG BOSS. So when I was told I had a meeting with him I was slightly shitting it. Usually us night-time people were left alone, so I was racked with anxiety. This is serious, I thought. Caroline said it had to be at her office, not Radio 1. Really serious. And it was to be at 9 a.m. and I couldn't be late: OK I'm dead.

I spent the day hassling Caroline about moving the meeting later and harassing her about what it was going to be about. She reassured me I was not going to be fired by saying, 'I don't think he would come to fire you face to face at 9 a.m.' I didn't believe her and continued worrying about what I was going to do for work. The next day rolls around and I set off for the meeting. Being a night owl meant I'd never left the house in rush hour before, so I was shocked that all these other people were trying to get into Soho for 9 a.m. on a weekday – what's everyone doing so early, I thought! There was nowhere to park and I had to ditch the car a street away at about 9.40 a.m. and leg it to the office. I hit the buzzer, ran up the stairs flustered, red and exhausted and gulped down a glass of water like a marathon runner, ready for my early-morning firing.

With no chance for pleasantries, I flopped into the sofa and genuinely said, 'Sorry I'm late; I am terrible in the morning.'

My agents Francis and Caroline put their heads in their hands. Now little did I know at the time, but this meeting was NOT the meeting to say that in. I wasn't going to be fired like I thought I was. Actually the complete opposite. It was to be THE meeting where Big Boss Ben offered me the Breakfast show.

SORRY

I'M

LATE

I

AM

TERRIBLE

IN

THE

MORNING

Not the sentence Big Boss Ben had imagined hearing today.

'Ahh, sorry to hear that because I want you to host the Breakfast show,' said Big Boss Ben.

'Oh! Shit! OK!' I replied 'I mean, really, wow, what?' My life was flashing before my eyes as I tried to take in what was happening. 'Really?' I asked again.

'Really,' he said.

So it was done. It was the quickest meeting I've ever had. I left after being sworn to secrecy, collected my parking ticket from the windscreen and texted a simple egg emoji to my nearest and dearest. They knew what I meant. My dream was to be realised.

It was the summer of 2012 and the feeling of possibility was in the air. It was a magical year and London felt like the centre of the universe. The Olympics were here and, as Radio 1's Big Weekend descended on Hackney with Jay-Z, Rihanna, Nicki Minaj and Kanye West in tow, we felt right at the heart of it all.

As often throughout my life, I felt it was my duty to throw a party. I wanted to do something to mark this momentous occasion of Jay-Z being in the park where we now walk our dogs. I rented Andi Oliver's pub on Columbia Road, a proper East End boozer with tiles all around it and a central bar like *EastEnders*. I booked DJs and asked Azealia Banks to come and perform, and she did '212' to a rapturous crowd of drunk Radio 1 staff. Then Rihanna herself turned up and no one knew what to do. We were all looking at each other with eyes that said:

OMG

RIHANNA

IS

AT

THE
PUB

as the kids from the houses nearby banged on the windows because the bass from our sound system made them rattle. My soon-to-be Breakfast producer Matt ran over to let me know Rihanna was here, not realising she was in earshot; she defo heard us screaming in excitement like little girls outside.

That was the end of June. I was to take over in September; just as kids and uni students were going back to a schedule, I too was going to have a new one. A new schedule that would change my sleeping habits, my career and ultimately my life. I thought it best to get a few days away in the sun to relax before I started. So I packed my bags and headed off to the very relaxing isle of Ibiza. What could go wrong? Well, quite a lot actually.

I had great intentions for the trip: I'd be productive, I'd plan out my first six months on Breakfast, I'd figure out features, think about guests, I'd read Chris Evans's book. I did at least attempt to do one thing from the list: I picked up Chris's book and read it – up to the point where he said he didn't really plan anything. I loved him with all my heart and trusted his broadcasting prowess above all others, so I put the book down and focused on my tan. If Chris doesn't plan, why should I? Then I got very, very thirsty and proceeded to go out-out rather than relaxing, arguing that this was representative of what the other young people of the UK were doing right now, so actually getting paralytic in DC10 was really kind of research.

'I don't think Radio 1 shows should be too planned anyway,' I said to Aimee, my friend who was there with me.

'Nah, fuck it. You don't wanna overthink it,' she said.

Sound advice.

But I had a big job on my hands. The Breakfast show is seen as the shop window to the rest of a radio station. I was taking over from Chris Moyles, and not only was he a man who had been on air for eight solid years, but tonally we couldn't have been more different. Yes, both northern, and yes, both love the sound of our own voices, but apart from that the change felt seismic. Moyles was brash, and controversial, and he made the papers when he'd seemingly overstep the mark. He was a DJ employed pre-social media; YouTube wasn't invented when he was given the reins of Breakfast, there was no Instagram, no Spotify, no Apple Music and certainly no TikTok. The world was a different place and Radio 1 were the big powerful bastards who set the scene for culture, music and conversation, hence why Little Me was so obsessed. But the times were a-changing and Radio 1 needed to change too.

Employing the 27-year-old from night-times was a statement of intent – they wanted people over thirty to stop listening. They needed the shop window to look different. Like Dr Who, we had to regenerate for a new generation, we started to do crazzzzyyyy things like FILM THE RADIO. I was holding a poisoned chalice in my hands; radio was being reinvented for the digital generation and I was at the heart of it, and initially the reaction wasn't that nice to experience.

I had visions of it being a huge success, of being just like it was in hedonistic 1996 when I'd been hooked on radio. Except it wasn't 1996 any more. In reality, the only way the figures could go were down. Big Boss Ben told me this was his strategy, that Radio 1 had a job to do: appeal to the kids, get them hooked into the BBC from an early age. They wanted to shake it up, chop the age range, lose listeners who were not relevant and prove to the BBC Trust that Radio 1 was a youth-focused brand.

Even so when the first set of listening figures came in and they'd gone down, it was nauseating. Like failing an exam. Well worse than that, cos the whole world saw your results then tweeted you: 'haha you're crap.'

I was uneasy. It was an incomprehensible experience: making your childhood dream come true (great!) and then being told you were shit at it by the nation (not great!). I felt like I'd let everyone down. I'd dread walking through the office. I felt the work of the 150 people in there was all for nothing, all their efforts in marketing, PR and production ruined because of me. I'd cringe through the corridors hoping not to make eye contact with anyone, and try to get out before the office filled up.

Then on my way home feeling like I'd let down the 150 people in the office, I'd worry about a few other people. About 61 million people actually. I knew the power of that Breakfast show, I remember how it anchored my mornings growing up, how it shaped and shifted my mood – and now that was my job. And I'd evidently put everyone in a shitty mood, because they'd stopped listening. I started to worry that people were having a shit morning – because of me – that would lead to a shit day for them and their lives would turn to shit because I was being shit at my job. And when your job is your personality, I summarised it (quite dramatically) as:

MY

TERRIBLE

PERSONALITY

IS

RUINING

GREAT

BRITAIN.

GREAT! My horrible personality has ruined everyone's lives. Those thoughts would fester and marinate in my brain for twenty-four hours, then I'd wake up and do it again the next day. Then I'd forget about it for a while and think fuck it, we're having fun and everyone can't like everyone! Then the figures came round again – they were quarterly – so I'd be on this rickety, life-or-death rollercoaster ride, riding out my emotions of agony and ecstasy. The ecstasy of getting to do my dream job every day, the agony of a builder saying, 'YER SHIT MATE' as I got out of my car at 6 a.m.

I don't know if the bosses were being polite or lying, but they said they were happy with the show and happy with the figures. That was the plan, they said. Surely not, I thought. The bosses wanted to take this risk. They said I was surely the only DJ in history who was employed to make audiences smaller. Rude! But it worked. Radio 1 became this beast of content, no longer a wireless analogue stream into our Fiestas but a multimedia megacorp copied by stations the world over. Radio had changed; but my need to connect with peoplé had remained.

I loved Breakfast so much. I loved planning the show and then having a nonsensical text derail it. I loved guests coming in hungover or still up. But most of all I cherished the warmth of strangers in the street. Everyone had an opinion on the show. Everywhere I went people spoke to me about it, picking up conversations that I'd had three days ago on air in Tesco: 'You're right about what you said to Jenny the caller the other day.'

I'd be racking my brains trying to remember what I'd said to Caller Jenny.

Once we'd ridden the Moyles changeover period we found our groove.

It was a constant feeling of go-go-go and I loved it. Fridays were the big day on the show, when big guests would come in with their world premieres of new music. I work best under pressure and so the times when all eyes and ears were on our show and the execs were sweating slightly was when I came alive; I lived for the drama of it all. There wasn't time to breathe and I could write a book on radio stories and guests alone. Every fucker came in – Kim Kardashian, Denzel Washington, Naomi Campbell, Dolly Parton, David Attenborough, you name them, they came on. It became weirdly normal that David Beckham was on the show and Stella McCartney, Chris Martin and Kate Winslet would text in for shout-outs on the school run. Even David Bowie asked me to premiere his new song to the world but unfortunately it was not a priority for Radio 1 at that time; we had real artists to play like Maroon 5 and Macklemore.

Breakfast was the greatest gift I'd ever received and it came from strangers, on the other end of this radio that had drawn me in as a kid. It made me realise how much I love British people and the contributions they made to not only the show but also to my own mental healing; they were a tonic I needed to down like a shot. I thought I'd have two years, or maybe three if I was lucky. In the end it was a month short of 6 years of 5 a.m. alarm clocks. Enough was enough. Over the course of the nearly six years I had started to fall in love with mornings, to enjoy the routine, the task of being up and at 'em with the bin men and birdsong. But what now? I never thought about what I'd do after Breakfast.

I was offered a dream show named after the worst phrase in radio: 'drive time'.

DRIVE

TIME!

TIME

TO

DRIVE!

It always makes me think of dads. Anyway, terrible name aside, it was a great gig. Great time, no alarm clock, I still got to do a daily show and I got to hand over to Annie Mac every evening.

From the minute I started my very first drive-time show I knew it would be the last I did for Radio 1. It felt full circle. It actually felt like I was drawing over and over the same circle and I needed to get out and draw another circle somewhere.

Then the pandemic hit and time stopped, it felt like everything stopped – apart from radio. All the staff were removed from the building so we could broadcast alone in hellish safety. The thrill of the packed office in the packed building in a packed city had gone, but radio remained constant. In a time away from family, friends and any social interactions, radio stopped me from going mad. It gave me something to do other than make sodding banana bread, it gave me focus and, most importantly, perspective. I was always grateful to be at Radio 1, but as I rode my bike through the deserted London streets each day, passing the odd key worker, I felt the weight of how lucky I was. Had I believed in God I would have high-fived him. Those bike rides into my childhood dream became emotional, life-affirming pilgrimages of gratitude. I was overjoyed at not only being out of the house, but also working, doing something I had always loved and still loved. Even at this culturally dead moment. In fact it mattered more than ever, the regularity and routine of it. The fear and uncertainty in the air meant I felt vulnerable on air, with four hours to fill on very little lols. There was no fun news, I'd done nothing fun, the listeners had done nothing fun, no celebrities had done anything fun, there was no sport on and we didn't really want to talk about Covid deaths, so we just had to exist. We just had to be.

It was a welcome vulnerability, a freeing one, which also allowed me to be more open than ever and to talk honestly about my fears and how I missed my family. The listeners opened up too, with us all feeling closer together than ever before, and I found beauty in simple conversation. It was a welcome comedown from the high-octane ride of my past fourteen years of broadcasting. I found solace in the simplicity of song, the power of hearing something requested by someone who was feeling a certain way, needing the music to do the talking for them. Just like I did all those years ago listening to Simon Bates in Eileen's Fiesta.

Then it was time to leave. Like with all my teenage obsessions – David Beckham and backwards Kangol hats – I, too, had started to fall out of love with Radio 1. And there was nothing David, Kangol or the BBC could do about it. I was just ready for another crush, another hat and another place to be. Actually I never wore another hat ever again. My head isn't right for hats. This isn't about hats!!

I felt like I'd done it. It was done. A feeling that had managed to be elusive throughout my life washed over me: a feeling of pure, reassuring contentment. The feeling you get when you finish a nice packet of crisps and think to yourself as you fold the bag, Mmmm that was nice.

It was the only time in my life I hadn't asked ten people for their opinion on something. Once I made the decision to go I told my mum. She was shocked. 'What? What you gonna do every day??' she asked.

I told her that I didn't know just yet and that most presenters don't work EVERY day anyway and I've been incredibly lucky to work there for fourteen years!

'Who doesn't work every day?'

'I dunno!' I said, racking my brain for an example. 'Claudia Winkleman!'

'She's got Head & Shoulders! She doesn't need to!'

Shit. She does, I thought. I tried Our Jane for another perspective.

'It will be invigorating,' she said.

And it was exactly that. Like a shower during a bad hangover, it was truly invigorating.

But what happens when the dream ends? What now? Never thought about this bit. Maybe I'll write a book?

Acknowledgements

Thank you to Caroline Ridley who I met one day for a coffee in Soho as a smelly infant of a man. I was doing bits of telly and I wanted to do radio, so Channel 4 suggested I need an agent and lined up meetings with various people. I met Caroline first and decided she was The One. She asked me about my dreams as she chain smoked her way through a packet of fags before putting her final one out and saying, 'OK let's do it then.' And we really did. Caroline grew to be more than an agent. She is a friend, a very stern second mother and fountain of knowledge, guidance and – essential when working with me – patience. I'd like to thank Caroline for guiding me out of Camden dive bars and through my dream career at the BBC and out the other side and into Hodder. Thank you for taking me (after a fag and a coffee on their doorstep) to meet the publishing gang and also thank you for constantly hassling me in such a way that sounds like you're not mad at my tardy chapter deadlines. When I know you're actually seething and it's driving you fucking mad. I hope you never leave me alone.

Also a massive thank you the entire Money Management team who are truly brilliant, making everything just seemingly happen seamlessly. I always feel so supported, so thank you. And of course our leader and commander Mr Money himself, Francis, thank you for always having my back, for making my ideas and dreams come to life, for listening to me whine, for putting up with my attention span and for your dedication to trying to bring back smoking indoors. It's never gonna happen! But I admire your passion.

Jonathan Hackford aka Mr 'Hey Mr!' Thank you for saying you liked my book more than most of the drivel you have to read for work purposes. I think that's a compliment? Thank you for your guidance and care over the years, I really appreciate it.

Writing a book made me shit myself with panic, it was something that kept me awake at night with dread thinking, how can I get out of this? Thank you to Lauren Whelan at Hodder who made me feel normal and my feelings valid. Lauren was the one who bribed me to write with milk chocolate hobnobs. Like an ageing donkey chasing a carrot, I plodded along following the delicious crumbs to our final published destination. Thank you for listening to all my paranoid panics and days of writer's block and understanding how my brain works. I'll always remember you saying, 'It's brilliant. Mad. But brilliant,' and thinking OK maybe she likes it.

Also, massive thank you to Kate Craigie at Hodder who, once Lauren DESERTED ME FOR A BABY!!!, took over my very much needed hand-holding. I love that I found a companion who likes reading from REAL paper and using pens like they used to in the olden days (pre the 2000s). I loved our days sat up on the roof with you trying not to strangle me for my inability to make a decision on literally anything. And your ability to happily respond to me at all times across all mediums: email, text, Zoom and WhatsApp. Sometimes all four at once.

Zakirah Alam is hands down the most organised, efficient, on-it person I have ever encountered. I felt like I worked at NASA or something watching you work. Now that the book is out, please can you take over running the country? You'd have it sorted by lunch.

Laura Weir: my truth-sayer editor who cracked up crying with laughter at one page before saying 'no, that bit is shit' as I read aloud onto the next page. Your honesty has been vital to me being happy with this book. You made me confident in my voice, in my writing and your very brutal and essential editing was top notch – 'Yehhh, said that bit before babe, DELETE!' I loved spending the days with you, drinking Skin Tea and eating chocolate as you listened to my every word about every day of my life. Hated you for the 3 minutes that you accidentally deleted a chapter. But we found it and I loved you again.

Thank you to Alice Morley and Becca Mundy from Marketing and Publicity who got me all wound up and excited from the minute I stepped foot into Hodder. You made me feel so welcome and so excited. And then scared that it was going to be a real thing that real people would really read.

All of you honestly made my anxieties melt away and now I'm sad I have no reason to come to annoy you at Hodder HQ.

Unless you want another?

Index